# WORSHIP ANEW IN BABYLON

## Community and Personal Worship Resources

**CLAUDE DOUGLAS BRYAN**

Despite the title, *Worship Anew in Babylon* taps into the very sap that runs throughout the ecumenical tree of our Christian faith. While Dr. Bryan draws from his Baptist branch of the tree, he engages the historic church and the seasons of human life. It is a joy to have this book, to ponder its content, and then put it to use.

Dr. Bryan jumps headlong into the challenge of remaining faithful to Christ in the exile brought by our religious and secular culture wars. His work presents us with prayers, storytelling, questions, poetry, and hymns meant to center us on our shared life in the great cloud of witnesses.

Yes, this is a resource for ministers and those leading congregational worship, but in addition, it gives any Christian useful tools to engage in worship beyond church walls for a world that so desperately needs something different, something holy—the people empowered by the Holy Spirit through the love of God in the grace of Jesus Christ.

— Rev. Drew Mangione,
pastor of Shelby Presbyterian Church, Shelby, NC


Doug Bryan has very thoroughly and systematically put together worship helps for a wide range of seasons and situations; from traditional church year seasons to particular community and/or congregational celebrations. Many, if not all, of these helps can be used by a variety of denominations, especially those of the free church tradition. In each section there are not only worship helps but there is also food for thought that will stimulate one's own creativity and ideas for a particular observance. Doug has dedicated a lifetime to church and church education. These pages are offered as an opportunity to deepen one's dedication to thoughtful worship.

—Rev. Candy Burch Wilson, having served Baptist, Disciples of Christ and United Methodist churches, is the Minister of Music and Visitation Pastor at Aldersgate United Methodist Church, Shelby, N.C.

# Dedicated to

Dr. Allen Graves Reed, beloved friend and colleague who taught me how to express thoughts  that could be sung to familiar tunes;

All who find themselves living and worshipping anew in Babylon;

And to

Those places and people who offer acceptance to all.

# Contents

# Preface

Of all the areas of church life and ministerial leadership, few are as challenging as the role of creator and leader of congregational worship. On the surface, it seems so simple—a hymn or two, a little Bible reading, some I-talk/you-talk leader-group interactions, and we're ready for a sermon. It seems simple both in its planning and execution. And it's almost always a one-sided activity—the leader "acts" and the worshippers passively respond.

Yet it is clear to most pastors and to many congregants that when worship on the Lord's Day turns into a cliché, as it often does, it becomes dreary and monotonous. What most pastors know, too, is that worship itself does *not* have to be dreary or monotonous. It is intended, as biblical text and church history both teach us, to be lively and engaging, active and God-centered—experienced deeply within one's soul. When that happens, nothing is more uplifting or humanly engaging than a collection of believers worshipping their God.

Achieving this, though, is not easy, nor is it automatic in any way, as every good pastor knows. It often requires someone to point the way toward creative, challenging, and vigorously spiritual Christian worship. That "someone" in this case is clearly Dr. Doug Bryan, whose new book/workbook meets every congregational need as a path to lively, engaging worship on a regular weekly basis.

This unique book is built around virtually all of the classic landmarks of the church's worship history, while at the same time giving them fresh language settings, creative forms of response, and strikingly original combinations of material from which creative worship leaders can draw. Dr. Bryan's understanding of and sensitivity to the nuances of church tradition and teaching are everywhere in these pages; and his weaving together of both new and old worship patterns will keep any formal worship service always new.

Dr. Bryan knows church and liturgical history. Moreover, he knows the patterns and meanings of virtually every major denominational tradition. This book is easily adapted for use in any praise or worship setting, large or small. Probably most important, this book—a ready "handbook" for weekly use—is *practical* for the preparation and leading of Christian worship, however the act of worship is defined or interpreted. What Dr.

Bryan has captured in these remarkable pages are ideas and guidelines that will add new life and sparkle to any congregational worship gathering. This book, in short, will give church congregants another reason to actively rejoice in Christian worship every Lord's Day.

Joseph M. Webb, PhD, DMin
Gardner-Webb University
Former President, Academy of Homiletics
July 1, 2022

# Biblical Admonitions on Exile

*We hanged our harps upon the willows in the midst thereof. For there they that carried us away captive required of us a song; and they that wasted us required of us mirth, saying, Sing us one of the songs of Zion. How shall we sing the LORD's song in a strange land?*
—Psalm 137:2-4

*Thus saith the LORD of hosts, the God of Israel, unto all that are carried away captives, whom I have caused to be carried away from Jerusalem unto Babylon; Build ye houses, and dwell in them; and plant gardens, and eat the fruit of them; Take ye wives, and beget sons and daughters; and take wives for your sons, and give your daughters to husbands, that they may bear sons and daughters; that ye may be increased there, and not diminished. And seek the peace of the city whither I have caused you to be carried away captives, and pray unto the LORD for it: for in the peace thereof shall ye have peace.*
—Jeremiah 29:4-7

*Peter, an apostle of Jesus Christ, to the strangers scattered throughout Pontus, Galatia, Cappadocia, Asia, and Bithynia,*
*Elect according to the foreknowledge of God the Father, through sanctification of the Spirit, unto obedience and sprinkling of the blood of Jesus Christ: Grace unto you, and peace, be multiplied. …And if ye call on the Father, who without respect of persons judgeth according to every man's work, pass the time of your sojourning here in fear.*
—1 Peter 1:1-2, 17

# Introduction

Exile can assume different forms, involving different persons and places. Stories of banishment and exile abound in human history. Whether it be individuals, families, nations, or religious faith groups, people, voluntarily or involuntarily, are in exile. In the biblical account found in Genesis, Adam and Eve were exiled from the Garden of Eden. Disobedience led to their exile into a new way of living. Their son Cain was exiled from his home. Taking his brother's life led to his wanderings. Abram followed God away from his home in a type of spiritual exile and journey from the past into a new future. The favored Joseph was sold into slavery and exile by his brothers' jealousy. The kingdom of Judah was defeated and taken into exile by the Babylonian Empire. The child Jesus went to Egypt, a place of safety and exile from the anger of Herod, until it was safe to return. John on the island of Patmos was in exile.

Differences in religious faith and tradition have created divisions that sent the minority into exile. The Jewish people were exiled from the Iberian Peninsula for failing to adopt Catholicism. The Huguenots left France to escape Catholic persecution, venturing into the New World. Roger Williams, a Puritan minister, was exiled by religious authorities from the Massachusetts Bay Colony to Rhode Island among more friendly Native Americans. Anne Hutchinson, a Puritan religious reformer, was exiled from Boston and found shelter in the wilderness. Under Catholic Queen Mary, Protestants in England sought exile; in turn, under Protestant King James I, Catholics in England sought safety in exile. These stories would continue.

While exile has traditionally been associated with relocation, exile can often be of an existential nature where one is no longer comfortable or understanding of new social mores and values. What once "fitted" no longer "fits." Simply stated, we cannot believe what we see and what we hear. How do we respond? Do we push back, pull back, or pull away? We are in exile.

Exile continues today as people of faith disagree on the power and truth of science. Ethical standards and values create debate among people of faith. Differences on the nature of the Bible and interpretation of Scripture further divide and fracture communities of faith. Fear of rejection and loss of community cause people to remain silent to the injustices and false claims they encounter.

Today, we see a land that is full of contradictions and displeasures. While we may have assumed that the rights of the citizenship are firmly held in place, we are learning that even these rights must be guarded, protected, reexamined, and expanded. We may have thought prejudice and discrimination were themes of the past, but we have learned that these are rampant today. While we enjoy the benefits of scientific advancement, we show resistance to vaccines designed to prevent or minimize disease. Welcoming of immigrants to the United States, though never perfect, has created increasing tensions, protests, and violence. Individual rights are preeminent over community rights. We argue about American citizenship. Civil discourse is a rarity. Tribalism and a new religious nationalism have emerged. These conditions are pleasing to some and frightening to others. Will we bring back, take back, or move forward?

On the first page of his work *A Tale of Two Cities*, Charles Dickens's description of eighteenth-century life sounds uncomfortably familiar:

> It was the best of times, it was the worst of times, it was the age of wisdom, it was the age of foolishness, it was the epoch of belief, it was the epoch of incredulity, it was the season of Light, it was the season of Darkness, it was the spring of hope, it was the winter of despair, we had everything before us, we had nothing before us, we were all going direct to Heaven, we were all going direct the other way—in short, the period was so far like the present period, that some of its noisiest authorities insisted on its being received, for good or for evil, in the superlative degree of comparison only. (Charles Dickens, *A Tale of Two Cities*, Project Gutenburg, https://archive.org/details/ataleoftwocities07869gut)

Though appropriate to the revolutionary seventeenth- and eighteenth-century world it describes, this description may be an accurate mirror of our present age.

It is in this context that *Worship Anew in Babylon* was created with the hope of providing encouragement, insight, and discussion as we learn to live, even prosper, and to sing songs of praise and worship in our times of exile. Exile is a time of new thoughts, understandings, revelations, and actions. Learning to live anew in exile and banishment is necessary. Exile involves our past—what we have left behind; our present—how we will live today; and our future—what our legacy will be. New questions arise. Is the golden rule still golden? Or is the golden rule merely gilded? What of the words of Mordecai to Esther concerning her role at the royal court? Have we been brought into the world for such a time as this (Esther 4:14)?

In closing, we should contemplate the words and the prayer, "For Those Who Come After Us," of Walter Rauschenbusch in his book *For God and the People: Prayers of the Social Awakening* (1910).

O God, we pray thee for those who come after us, for our children, and the children of our friends, and for all the young lives that are marching up from the gates of birth, pure and eager, with the morning sunshine on their faces. We remember with a pang that these will live in the world we are making for them. We are wasting the resources of the earth in our headlong greed, and they will suffer. We are building sunless houses and joyless cities for our profit, and they must dwell therein. We are making the burden heavy and the pace of work pitiless, and they will fall wan and sobbing by the wayside. We are poisoning the air of our land by our lies and our uncleanness, and they will breathe it. O God, thou knowest how we have cried out in agony when the sins of our fathers have been visited upon us, and how we have struggled vainly.

Save us from maiming the innocent ones who come after us by the added cruelty of our sins. Help us to break the ancient force of evil by a holy and steadfast will and to endow our children with purer blood and nobler thoughts. Grant us grace to leave the earth fairer than we found it; to build upon it cities of God in which the cry of needless pain shall cease; and to put the yoke of Christ upon our business life that it may serve and not destroy. Lift the veil of the future and show us the generation to come as it will be if blighted by our guilt, that our lust may be cooled and we may walk in the fear of the Eternal. Grant us a vision of the far-off years as they may be if redeemed by the sons of God, that we may take heart and do battle for thy children and ours. (Walter Rauschenbusch, *For God and the People: Prayers of the Social Awakening*, 1910, https://archive. org/details/forgodandthepeop00rausuoft)

# Prologue

Have you ever found yourself in "Babylon"? My usage of Babylon means any place where you don't want to be; places that you don't understand; places where irrationality seems dominant; places where the absurd becomes the norm; places where you imagine nothing could be more ridiculous, and then you discover that it can and does get more ridiculous. As depicted in the biblical narrative, Babylon is a place of exile. It is a place of discouragement where you must learn to live all over again. "How shall we sing the LORD's song in a strange land" (Psalm 137:4)?

The COVID-19 pandemic has been one of the indicators that we are living in exile in a new Babylon filled with necessary safety measures, vaccinations, working from home, limited in-person social interactions, and more students engaged in remote learning. Babylon is also where religious communities are divided, even among smaller churches. While the division may be political in origin, these differences destroy what at one time appeared to be united communities of faith. Faith is superseded by other loyalties. Mistrust prevails—disenfranchised members; divided families; split membership; hurt feelings; harsh words; departing ministerial staff; and a lack of respect and basic civility.

This is Babylon, a time of exile from the past and an opportunity to rethink what has happened and envision what is to come. The pandemic began as I started my retirement. Most of my activities have been housebound. Two of my most precious projects have been reading and collecting. One specific focus has been reading about the faith traditions and practices of other groups within the Christian faith community. My appreciation has increased for the varying communities with both commonality and uniqueness across the centuries. My collecting involved compiling my various writings, especially hymns, that I have done over the decades. No single identified location housed "my treasures." I only knew that once I departed the earth, these writings would be lost forever. Like the Jews of Babylon, I collected my literary endeavors for preservation.

What I discovered during the pandemic involved the gift of reflection I was afforded. I have been able to rethink thoughts that I once easily took for granted. I suspect this opportunity was also presented to the exiled Jews as a time to collect, to reflect, and to refine their heritage.

This book is offered to church leadership responsible for setting the stage for congregational worship. It includes writings in a mixture of both content and style. Some language is more traditional and other language is more contemporary. The hymns are set to meter that is in the public domain. Leaders will find a variety of readings including responsive readings, prayers, monologues, catechisms, poems, choral readings, and more. The content of each chapter includes a precis, hymns, readings, stories and theological reflections, and a seasonal prayer. Numerous questions are intermingled with the readings and stories. Various sayings, ideas, and quotations are provided to provoke thought and reflections, even if originating from those of different faiths, genders, historical periods, and ethnicities. We can learn from all, even those whose "hometown" might be Babylon.

The book is divided into "times"—typical themes, events, or activities found within the church calendar. Material that appears in one season may be used at other times. Arranged alphabetically, these times are the moments that are both planned and unexpected within the dynamic life of a typical congregation. Those who read these pages may find resources for both devotional and personal growth as well as for public worship. These pages are based on subjective experiences, creativity, and theological reflections—and sometimes all three combined into one. One of my goals is to help readers experience new imaginations, reflections, and actions.

Unless otherwise noted, the biblical texts are from the King James Version of the Bible. These materials are intended for educational and worship-related events. Every effort has been made to ensure that the suggested hymn tunes are in the public domain. Both the meter and suggested tunes are listed with the hymns. These tunes are found in commonly used hymnals. You may also find the hymn tunes at www.hymnary.org or other web sites to determine if the music can be used within copyright law. Should you utilize any hymn, poem, readings, prayer, etc., please include the author's name.

Quotations attributed to various individuals and groups at the beginning of each section were found in internet sources without benefit of the original source.

I hope these resources will add new seasonings to the various times, occasions, and themes of a typical church year. Should you agree that you, too, are living in some type of Babylon, I hope these words will give hope, encouragement, and inspiration in uncertain and challenging days.

# Times of Advent to Christmas

*And the Word was made flesh, and dwelt among us, (and we beheld his glory, the glory as of the only begotten of the Father,) full of grace and truth.*
—John 1:14

*It is for us to see the Kingdom of God as always coming, always pressing in on the present, always big with possibility, and always inviting immediate action.*
—Walter Rauschenbusch

*Rejoice, that the immortal God is born,*
*so that mortal men may live in eternity.*
—Jan Hus

Weeks of preparation are moments away from being fulfilled in the celebrations of December 25. We've wrapped presents, written greetings, enjoyed Christmas music, planned meals, and decorated church and home. We've been reminded of our blessings and prosperity as we recall those whose lives are less fortunate. Many of the world's citizens are displaced, diseased, unemployed, grieving, and hungry. Whether it is in times of prosperity or despair, Advent and Christmas come. This time brings people back to the church to celebrate with extended families. Advent and Christmas give us pause to reflect on what we have gained and lost in the endings of the years. Promises are made at Christmas, some to be kept and others to be broken.

Like King David, we may reflect on our own prosperity and our desire to honor God at events like Christmas. A successful David desired to honor God with a house. Such houses of deity were common in David's day. For some, the house represented the deity's dwelling place. The house may also have represented the deity's endorsement of the authority of the political rulers. Another common theme of the day was the belief in the localization of the deity. Some deities were viewed as being strongest in specified locations.

In 2 Samuel 7:1-13, how surprised David must have been when Nathan brought the word that David was not to build the temple! The passage clearly teaches that Yahweh was not confined to one location, but Yahweh's presence had gone with the people on their journeys in the Promised Land. Politically and theologically, God was not to be too closely defined, localized, and controlled. In many respects, our understanding of the work of God is also limited and imperfect. A temple would be built but within God's time, plan, purpose, and person.

What theological irony! While David wanted to give God a house, God instead promised David a house (dynasty) that would be endless and not limited to one location. God's love would never depart from David's descendants. While David would experience the chastisement of a loving Father, God's love would be ever present.

Often, we are like David. We make plans and dream dreams. Yet God surprises us by making dreams beyond our limited imaginations a reality. So it is with Advent. We make the preparations in anticipation and in remembrance of the Savior's birth. In some respects, we try to make Christmas, but Christmas is an act of God. May we not get so lost in our own plans and expectations that we fail to wait, to listen, to watch, and to respond to God's person and work through Advent. Let us keep our minds, hearts, and eyes open to the surprises of God.

The following pages provide supplemental resources that might enhance preparation for the celebration of Christmas. You will find several hymns, readings, stories and theological reflections, and a seasonal prayer. May these resources become a seasoning to add new flavor to this important celebration wherever you might be. May you experience new imaginations, insights, and actions.

## We Celebrate Advent

**Claude Douglas Bryan**               **Suggested Tunes: ASH GROVE**
**KREMSER**
**Meter: 12.11.12.11.D.**

We celebrate Advent that leads us to Christmas,
Where sorrow and sadness on earth will soon pass,
By walking among us throughout the world's vexed day,
This young babe became the one showing God's way.

We celebrate Advent that leads us to Christmas,
Where brokenness finds your repairing at last,
With good news for each one, proclaiming God's true son,
Rejoicing at Christmas what Easter has won.

We celebrate Advent that leads us to Christmas,
Where God showed us love that sin could not surpass.
Belief in the Son brings renewal through rebirth,
Through sharing and making shalom on the earth.

We celebrate Advent that leads us to Christmas,
With evil's defeat by our God's mighty pass,
With good news for each one, proclaiming God's true son,
Rejoicing at Christmas what Easter has won.

We celebrate Advent that leads us to Christmas,
With worship and fellowship not bound by class.
The rich and the poor both renewed through God's power,
Found living as one in earth's holiest hour.

We celebrate Advent that leads us to Christmas,
Where Jesus was victor in battle, alas
With good news for each one, proclaiming God's true son,
Rejoicing at Christmas what Easter has won.

# Born to Show Us God's Great Love

**Claude Douglas Bryan**

**Suggested Tune: MENDELSSOHN**
**Meter: 7.7.7.7.D. with refrain**

Born to show us God's great love, love that finds and warms our soul;
Plan divine, both act and time, far beyond the earth's control;
Heart and life were broken still, finding not their perfect peace;
God made flesh so we might live, granting God's own sweet release;
Born to show us God's great love, love that finds and warms our soul.

Born to show us God's great love, love renews and heals our soul;
Promised Gift at last fulfilled, bringing back what sin once stole;
Humble setting, Christ, the babe, came to live and understand
Earthly life as one of us, off'ring peace throughout the land;
Born to show us God's great love, love renews and heals our soul.

Born to show us God's great love, love and life for ev'ry soul;
Christ the Savior he would grow, word and deed, a priceless toll;
Tempted, tried, and proven true, Jesus lived God's love for you;
Christmas joy and Easter's hope, life through death shall make us new;
Born to show us God's great love, love and life for ev'ry soul.

Born anew we now proclaim, love we share for ev'ry soul;
Let us sing this message true, Christ can make the broken whole;
May we join each other's pain, comfort found in Jesus name;
Let us work to live this love, till all know we are the same;
Born anew we now proclaim, love we share for ev'ry soul.

                                          

# Love Became the Royal Light

**Claude Douglas Bryan**

**Suggested Tunes: DIX**
**TOPLADY**
**Meter:** 7.7.7.7.7.7.

In a land of God's own choice,
Captives there could not rejoice,
Suffered under foreign scour.
God revealed in this his hour,
Held not comforts of the night.
Love became the royal light.

Time of darkness and of hate,
God's redemption came not late.
God removed once more our fear,
Should to we all draw near.
Christ was born on Christmas morn;
All to him we must adorn.

Show to us again today—
Living justice is your way.
In the darkness of this place,
God display your saving grace,
Christ alone can bring us near
With the One who loves us dear.

# Love Became the Royal Light (with refrain)

**Claude Douglas Bryan**

**Suggested Tune: MARTYN**
**Meter: 7.7.7.7.7.7.D.**

In a land of God's own choice,
Captives there could not rejoice,
Suffered under foreign scour.
God revealed in this his hour,
Held not comforts of the night.
Love became the royal light.
Love became the royal light,
Guiding journeys of the night.

Time of darkness and of hate,
God's redemption came not late.
God removed once more our fear,
Should to him we all draw near.
Christ was born on Christmas morn;
All to him we must adorn.
Love became the royal light,
Guiding journeys of the night.

Show to us again today—
Living justice is your way.
In the darkness of this place,
God, display your saving grace.
Christ alone can bring us near
With the One who loves us dear.
Love became the royal light,
Guiding journeys of the night.

# Like a Daily Sunrise (Poem)

Like a daily sunrise, a new year brings
Open fresh and new options and choices
With new restarts and chances for life's springs
To affirm, reclaim, and create new voices.

Past voices call us to the days ahead—
Live in the past or in the here and now.
What will we write on slates yet to be read?
What newness on clean slates will we allow?

## Questions to Ponder

1. The first stanza has an optimistic tone. Do all people have an expectancy of optimism for the future? What makes one optimistic or pessimistic about the future? Explain.
2. What is your reaction to the admonition, "Live in the past or in the here and now"?
3. What aspects of life need to be rewritten in your life, your family, or your community of faith? How can this rewriting be accomplished?

# Looking for the Christ (Poem)

Looking for the Christ of Bethlehem,
Born thousands of years ago,
Foretold by Jewish prophets,
Hidden hope of the oppressed,
Looking for the Christ of Bethlehem.

Looking for the Christ of Bethlehem,
The young One in the temple,
A runaway who stayed behind,
Questioning and amazing,
Looking for the Christ of Bethlehem.

Looking for the Christ of Bethlehem,
The One baptized by his cousin,
Welcomed by the oppressed,
Preaching, teaching, and healing,
Looking for the Christ of Bethlehem.

Looking for the Christ of Bethlehem,
The Mature One tempted,
Who said yes to what was destiny,
Bread, hope, and life,
Looking for the Christ of Bethlehem.

Looking for the Christ of Bethlehem,
Breaking through death,
Rising to new life for all,
No more looking and searching,
Having found the Christ of Bethlehem.

## Questions to Ponder

1. Have you looked for the Christ of Bethlehem? Explain.
2. What does the Christ of Bethlehem offer?
3. What difference does it make to find the Christ of Bethlehem?
4. If you were to write the next stanza of the poem, what would it be?

    

# Unwrapped Gifts

As usual, beneath the Christmas tree were plenteous, neatly wrapped packages. Each one offered a surprise to be opened on Christmas morning. With each passing year, the oldest child had grown more curious and courageous. Curiosity and courage gave way to impatience. Once everyone was asleep, he carefully crept downstairs and admired the brightly wrapped presents bearing his name. Why not? he thought. No one would know. He selected one package and carefully unwrapped it.

Wow, he thought. It's just what I wanted. For the next hour he played with the Christmas present behind the couch. When he thought he had better get to bed, he meticulously rewrapped the present and placed it in the original spot under the tree.

Cautiously, he repeated the procedure for several nights prior to Christmas. Each night, creeping while everyone was asleep, he would unwrap, open, play with, and rewrap the present. One night, he thought he heard a sound. He held his breath; his body froze. He heard nothing else. He must have been mistaken. He had gone through all his presents under the tree. Nothing was left. He must wait for Christmas morning and pretend to be surprised.

When Christmas morning came, he joined the family in their ritual of opening presents. When it was his turn to open one present, he mustered his dramatic skill to imitate a smile and entertain his family. He was sure that he could pull it off. He opened the package, discovering not the toy he wanted and expected but instead underwear and pajamas. So it was with each present he opened. His father read the genuine expression on his face and said, "It's nice to be surprised, isn't it, son?"

## Questions to Ponder

1. Should Christmas always be predictable?
2. How does Advent contribute to celebrations of Christmas?
3. Is surprise a part of the Christmas message? Explain.

## Anything but Peaceful

Cards declare the message of Christmas, songs call for its coming, and prayers ask for it to come. We associate Christmas with peace. Interestingly, Christmas has always involved conflict. An unconventional marriage. Probably neighborhood gossip. Conflict within the involved families. The context of the original Christmas was a couple traveling to be part of a census for taxation. No adequate housing. No record of health care to include a midwife. Plenty of political intrigue. The young couple became immigrants fleeing for the life of their baby, escaping the genocide of those babies left behind. It's not a simple story but a story of twists and turns. Anything but peaceful.

Centuries later, conflicts or differences still exist. The Eastern Church celebrates Christmas around January 7, the Western Church on December 25. Different customs and celebrations have occurred throughout history. December 25 has been regarded as a holy day, and other groups felt its celebration was wrong. The Pilgrims in New England worked on Christmas Day, thinking the observance had become too Catholic.

Families are divided on which set of in-laws to visit at Christmas. Children of divorced parents may be involved in shared custody and visitation. How do large families exchange gifts? What about the fairness of money spent on gifts? What should be the main meat served? What type of stuffing is best? Who has the best-decorated home in the neighborhood? How can we have Christmas that rivals the Christmas of our childhood? What topics of discussion are off-limits? Can Christmas be celebrated if you are not where you want to be?

Conflicts and competitions, some great and some small, occur every year at the celebration of Jesus' birth. Christmas calls us to messages of peace, wholeness, and wellness for everyone amid differences of opinion and preferences.

### Questions to Ponder

1. What are the origins of your associations with Christmas or your practices at Christmas? Explain.
2. Has commercialism hindered the message of Christmas? Explain.
3. Can Christmas be observed with both celebrations and solemnity? How?

 

                                                       

## God, the Author and Creator

God, both the author and creator of our faith, we thank you for fashioning each of us in your image. Keep us on the wonderful journey of discovering what it means to be in your image. May we live as your children. We are linked to you, to each other, and to the earth. We live as one created in your image, dwelling on your earth, your creation. Created to give and to receive love, we have opportunities to reveal this divine image to all creation. Advent is preparation for us to deepen the gift of life through Jesus the Christ.

We wait for you in places familiar and unfamiliar. We acknowledge that our lives may not be what we wish them to be. Regardless of places and circumstances, may this Advent season prepare us to recall the birth of the Christ child and the rebirth that is offered to each of us. Prepare us for life in the present and the life to come. May our lives show how love might be shared afresh in ways that honor the teachings of Jesus the Christ. Reveal what we must acknowledge; reveal from what we must turn away; reveal what we must embrace; and reveal how we should live and walk. Give us revelation. Grant to us measures of daily divine grace as we live in your presence and anticipate your fuller presence. In this season of waiting and celebrating, we pray in your holy name, Jesus the Crucified. Amen.

                    

# TIMES OF BAPTISM AND COMMUNION

*One lord, one faith, one baptism.*
—Ephesians 4:5


*The better we know Jesus, the more social do his thoughts and aims become.*
—Walter Rauschenbusch


*Baptism is an outward expression of an inward faith.*
—Watchman Nee

Baptism and Communion, or the Lord's Supper, are regarded as ordinances within my own faith tradition. Baptism is a public declaration of a decision to follow Jesus the Christ, the initiating public act of the Christian pilgrimage. The Lord's Supper is a continuing meal of remembrance. While these two observances may be regarded as symbolic, they represent powerful symbols that guide and orient our lives. They are living symbolic acts or dramas providing a living testimony of the Christian message, Christian community, and unity with God.

Regardless of the mode—sprinkling, affusion, or immersion—baptism signifies a new direction in the life of the individual. Baptism is a significant experience requiring thoughtfulness and commitment. In the ancient Christian world, baptism was often the result of a two- to three-year period of instruction for the one wishing to be baptized for full church membership. It signifies a carefully developed instructional movement from an old way of life to a new way of life. Within the Christian realm, at one time all children were baptized as infants into the Christian community. Later opportunity was given for individual confirmation of the baptismal promises made by their parents. Later in the Protestant world, baptism would emerge from infant baptism into believer's baptism.

The Eucharist, Communion, or the Lord's Supper is a commemorative meal in which individual members experience shared remembrance of the life, love, and sacrifice of Jesus the Christ. In community they are called together to recall the intent of oneness with Christ within community and oneness with each other. It is a holy moment of both human and divine interaction.

The Lord's Supper may be observed within the church throughout the church year. For some these observances may be weekly; for others it may be monthly or quarterly; for others occasionally. Regardless of the frequency, these acts dramatize the new life for individuals in the faith community. In the shared moments together, we each are afforded an opportunity to relive what Jesus did for us and to recommit to Jesus the Christ and his values. Baptism may begin the journey, and in the Lord's Supper we celebrate the journey with others.

The following pages provide supplemental resources that might enhance preparation for the celebration of baptism and the Lord's Supper.

You will find several hymns, readings, stories and theological reflections, and a seasonal prayer. May these resources become a seasoning to add new flavor to these important celebrations. May you experience new imaginations, insights, and actions.

# Amidst Great Wealth or Poverty

**Claude Douglas Bryan**         **Suggested Tunes: ES FLOG EINKLEINS**
**WALDVOGELEN**
**Meter: 7.6.7.6.D.**

Amidst great wealth or poverty, in rooms both bare and grand,
Our numbers may be large or few, we follow God's command.
God's welcome calls us homeward, with loving, patient reach;
We find God's table open, with room and place for each.

Forgiveness we find in this place, by Christ's own loving hand,
With no condemnation now, with hearts that understand.
Love lived in word and action, acceptance we each find;
May lives show truth and justice; God's grace makes each one shine.

Our sharing God's work on earth, all living with their part;
This witness shared in common, his love becomes our art;
Confession brings redemption, Good News for all to hear;
With broken bread and chalice, join God's communion here.

# Silence Grants Its Finest Wonder

**Claude Douglas Bryan**

**Suggested Tunes: RATHBURN**
**KINGDOM**
**Meter: 8.7.8.7.**

Silence grants its finest wonder;
Quiet times where God can speak;
Giving our eyes a chance to see
Darkness changing to new light.

Places open for the weary;
Places set for hungry ones;
Places set where you too may serve;
Places where you will be served.

Contemplation brings us power;
Honest words we now receive;
Truth received brings life and freedom;
Changed by power found in grace.

Places open for the weary;
Places set for hungry ones;
Places set where you may serve;
Places where you will be served.

Scripture claims the worldwide message:
Jew nor Gentile, we are one.
Welcomes given, home for each one,
We announce God's love for all.

# Cleansing Waters

**Claude Douglas Bryan**

**Suggested Tune: KINGDOM**
**Meter: 8.7.8.7.**

Cleansing waters call us homeward,
Jesus' love forever poured.
Showing word and deed display,
Justice found for all our days.

Follow him from days of birth;
Showing love to all on earth,
Healing love remakes us as one,
Our life's searching, we find done.

Breathing into life the world fresh;
Savior born in borrowed crèche;
Raised from death our benefit still;
Give to him our heart and will.

Asking bravely would you come near,
Calling waters beckon clear;
Come as we together give all,
Join this holy common call.

Jesus, we affirm, our true Lord,
Singing faith in one accord.
We embrace the heavenly host—
Father, Son, and Holy Ghost.

# Meals (Poem)

Meals bring families together,
Sharing the stories of the day,
Shielding us from outside danger,
Giving us strength along our way.

Meals shared as one in Jesus' name,
Sacred words of remembered love,
Reminding of the name we claim,
Joining each with the One above.

## Questions to Ponder

1. Apart from nutritional value, what is the value of shared meals?
2. What role do you believe shared meals play in the biblical narrative?
3. Do shared meals have value in our time? Explain.
4. Why do you think the Lord's Supper is considered sacred within the various Christian traditions?

# Baptismal and Congregational Pledge
## (Responsive Reading)

LEADER: Why have we gathered in this place?

**PEOPLE:** To give witness to the baptism of this (these) follower(s) of Jesus the Christ.

LEADER: [To the baptismal candidate(s)] What do you promise today?

*CANDIDATES:* We (I) promise to follow Jesus the Christ.

LEADER: What do you promise to this (these) candidate(s) for baptism?

**PEOPLE:** We promise to support them in their discipleship.

LEADER: Will you support them with time and encouragement?

**PEOPLE:** We will.

LEADER: [To the baptismal candidate(s)] Will you accept their time and encouragement?

*CANDIDATES:* We (I) will.

LEADER: How will you teach them to observe all things?

**PEOPLE:** We will teach them by example.

LEADER: The candidate(s) please come forward. Do you, (Name), accept Jesus Christ as your Lord and Savior?

*CANDIDATE:* I do.

LEADER: I baptize you, (Name), in the name of the Father, the Son, and the Holy Spirit. Buried with Christ in baptism and risen to new life. And the people of God said:

**PEOPLE:** Amen.

## Metaphors as Answers

A man approached the pastor of a local church. The man was from a different faith tradition. The pastor knew him as a family man who had all outward indications of a healthy family life. There were no rumors about the man or his integrity. The fellow had many questions about the practices of the church. He asked the pastor to explain baptism and the Lord's Supper. The pastor told him a story.

He had once counseled a young couple who came to him to ask about weddings and marriage. The pastor knew that both individuals had been reared in similar church traditions. They had been college sweethearts. They said they were committed to one another.

The pastor explained that a marriage was like a public baptism. He went on to say that the wedding ceremony, whether it be at city hall, in the backyard, at a destination wedding, or in the church sanctuary, was a public declaration of the couple's commitment to one another. At the conclusion of the ceremony, the couple became married and were so viewed by the public with all afforded rights and privileges of married couples. The couple had expressed public commitment and expectations to one another in a community context.

However, marriages are to be sustained by participation through time spent together in various relationships, the pastor explained. There would be times of shared work, shared physical intimacy, shared conversation, shared problem-solving, shared traveling, and shared disappointments. Each of the shared activities would offer opportunities for the couple to become closer to their original wedding vows. The shared activities would also remind them of the importance and priority of each other in this relationship.

The shared activities were an opportunity for the couple to say to each other, sometimes verbally and sometimes nonverbally, I love you and I am committed to you. These activities would increase the possibility for deeper and meaningful intimacy in all aspects of life. The couple would periodi-cally visit both sides of the family in such activities as graduations, reunions, Christmas activities, birthday dinners, and vacations. Each of these activi-ties would bind the couple to one another and to the extended family for a greater purpose and a stronger identity.

 

The pastor went on to share with the inquiring man of a different faith tradition how the commitment symbolized by marriage was a way to view the commitment symbolized by baptism and the Lord's Supper.

## Questions to Ponder

1. In what ways, if any, are baptism and a wedding ceremony similar?
2. How might baptism and wedding locations be similar?
3. In what ways, if any, are Communion (the Lord's Supper) and shared activities in a marriage similar?

# Dunking

Baptists are known for baptism by immersion and, more importantly, believer's baptism. Considered enemies by Catholics and Protestants, the Baptists were known as "Dunkers." Reared in the Methodist church, my wife-to-be became involved with a group of students known at that time as the Baptist Student Union. Her fellow friends expressed concern about her baptismal experience within her Methodist church. Her baptism had been by sprinkling as an infant, and she had received confirmation as an adolescent.

Years later, my wife-to-be and I would meet and marry. In her family, there were some elements of concern about Julie's marrying a Baptist or a Dunker. While Julie had become a Baptist in college, I suppose they thought the marriage would forever be tied to the group of Baptists.

How did Julie become a Baptist? The questions people asked about her baptism initiated reflections. Julie took action. Julie requested that her Methodist pastor at a Methodist church camp baptize her by immersion in the lake. Weeks later, Julie joined a Baptist church without need for future baptisms. When she and I talked about her experience, I asked why she had wanted a Methodist pastor to perform a baptism by immersion. She said her friends had questioned the validity of her mode of baptism, and she did not want to be an obstacle to them. Julie voluntarily chose to be rebaptized. If they questioned the baptism being conducted by a Methodist pastor, the problem was theirs, not hers. I wish that I possessed her maturity and her insight.

When her parents retired, they moved to be near us and, most important, their two grandsons. Her parents attended the Baptist church where we were members. When we moved across the country, they followed us once more and attended for multiple years the Baptist church where we moved our membership. They attended, they participated, and they tithed to the church, but they were not members. In their eighties, they were baptized by immersion to join the Baptist church. I stood in the baptismal waters with them as the minister baptized them. The officiating minister emphasized that this baptism was for membership within the church requirements. In no way was this immersion a declaration against the validity of their previous baptisms, Methodist church involvement, and Christian experience.

## Questions to Ponder

1. How important is baptism to the individual and to the church? Explain.

2. What comments would you make about Julie's decision to be baptized by immersion?

3. Do baptism requirements hinder the involvement of adults who come from other church traditions?

4. Should baptism be reexamined?

# God Revealed in Jesus the Crucified

God revealed in Jesus the Crucified, be with us in this invitation into the lives of others. Baptismal waters mark a turning point, a reaffirmation, of our desire to live under your direction and guidance. We are each born into the human family; we each are given an open invitation to claim your love and your forgiveness. Let these waters be a witness and a call to all who believe, who want to believe, and who have yet to believe. Just as a baby learns to walk in small steps, often falling and beginning again, we commit these individuals to your care as they learn to walk in your ways. We commit ourselves as we learn to support them in their journey. Lest [add names of baptismal candidates] stumble, let us be your hands to lift [add names] up and to begin again. We acknowledge that God who sustains these new ones [add names] is the one who sustains us as well. We are in these moments together, joining a great cloud of witnesses.

Baptism is God's invitation and our acceptance. While it may signify church membership, more importantly, may it be a testimony of our desire to commune with you, God, and with one another. Wash us fresh in the waters of forgiveness, of love, and of sustenance. May our souls be reborn once more into your kingdom of love and light. In the name of Jesus the Crucified, we pray. Amen.

 

# TIMES OF BENEVOLENCE AND JUSTICE

*But let judgment run down as waters, and righteousness as a mighty stream.*
—Amos 5:24


*Injustice anywhere is a threat to justice everywhere.*
—Martin Luther King Jr., *Letters from Birmingham Jail*

It is ironic, indeed, that we need to be reminded to continue to focus on benevolence and justice for all. For those of us born in the United States of America and for those who study to become citizens of this nation, these concepts are part of our founding civic documents. Those who are born again into God's Kingdom discover that these concepts are witnessed in the biblical record. To listen to the voice of Jesus as recorded in Scripture is to hear a call to kindness and justice toward all our neighbors.

While we may not have a special season or Sunday designated for benevolence and justice, periodically we may be called upon to emphasize these concepts as both words of remembrance and challenge. In fact, these themes should be periodically emphasized throughout the year. It is easy to become complacent and to assume benevolence and justice have been achieved. Because these things may be achieved for our own population group, we may erroneously assume that they have been achieved for all. We are wrong, and we may become complacent to the needs of others of different race, religion, and language.

Focus on the call of Scripture challenges our complacency and false sense of righteousness. We should listen to the story of Jesus' response to the scribes who asked the perennial question, "Who is my neighbor?" Through the Good Samaritan story (Luke 10:25-37) we discover that our neighbors are those who are in need. With advances in social media, it is easy to recognize that the neighbor has broadened to people beyond our immediate housing, neighborhood, church, friends, social sphere, or business circles. With expanded views of neighbor taught by Jesus, do we invest the time and resources to bring acts of benevolence and justice to those whom we may not personally encounter?

The following pages provide supplemental resources that might enhance the observation and promotion of benevolence and justice themes. You will find several hymns, readings, stories and theological reflections, and a seasonal prayer." May these resources become a seasoning to add new flavor to this important theme. May you experience new imaginations, insights, and actions.

 

# Our God in Christ Has Walked Earth's Way

**Claude Douglas Bryan**　　　　　　　　**Suggested Tune: ST. ANNE**
**Meter: 8.6.8.6.**

Our God in Christ has walked earth's way;
His life, the Potter's Clay.
By showing people courage true,
God's plan we come to view.

Transformed through God's restoring love,
New strength we find above;
Empowered life on earth anew
New acts of love we do.

Forgotten ones still call our name,
From places we once came;
God's love for them we must proclaim,
If true to Jesus' name.

With faithful justice shown for all,
This wonder of God's call,
We yearn to know more what is right,
And act with holy might.

With thanks to God we give our praise—
To sing and live our days.
With love and joy shown ev'rywhere,
We live as God's true heir.

# Behind the Lattice

**Claude Douglas Bryan**

**Suggested Tunes: ST. ANNE**
**ST. PETER**
**ST. AGNES**
**Meter: 8.6.8.6.**

Oh, God of Love and God of Might, reveal thy pure delight;
Thy mysteries we might discern; our joy to teach and learn.

Through days of ease and wealth with thee, may we not fail to see
The ones around us who lack hope, who feel beyond love's scope.

Behind the lattice may we see the ones with silent plea,
Who wait and watch and long to be reclaimed to life set free.

These hidden ones we must address with love and tenderness;
Our presence there is Christ's command, to walk beside their stand.

Uplifting lives becomes our task; to serve is what we ask;
May those on earth who need our care find justice that is fair.

May those we teach learn how to share grace gentle everywhere;
Lives taught through love touch others still with peace and God's good will.

# Forgotten Ones (Poem)

Forgotten ones still call our name,
From places we once came;
God's love for them we must proclaim,
If true to Jesus' name.

May those we teach learn to share,
Grace gentle everywhere;
Lives taught through love touch others still,
With peace and God's good will.

## Questions to Ponder

1. Whom do you believe the author is referring to with the phrase "forgotten ones"? Explain.
2. Can you identify individuals or groups of people who might be the "forgotten ones"? Explain.
3. How can we minister to the "forgotten ones"? Explain.
4. Do the "forgotten ones" minister to us? Explain.

## Born in the Year of Brown (Monologue)

Born in the year of Brown vs. Board of Education;
Separate but Equal was brought into question.
Equality for all with limited or controlled associations?
Southern Baptists campaigned for a "Million More in 54."
Who were the million evangelized to be?
Looking back, I am not always proud of the world in '54.
It was a black and cloudy world—but not because of skin color,
black because of the darkness of our heads and our hearts—
Injustice, Prejudice, Poverty, Bigotry, and Ignorance were ingrained in our
    very thought processes.
Our thinking patterns could not distinguish between light and darkness,
Between what should have been a simple right and wrong.
We thought and acted in our safe and secure stereotypes.
Cora was a real Black Woman, no stereotype.
Cora, our Maid, our Nurse, our Protector.
Cora kept three "wild" white children for $3.00 a day,
While our mother sewed buttons on the collars of oxford shirts.
Once Cora said these were slave wages—
Nobody paid by the day anymore but us, she said.
Fired and re-hired many times during the years—
On and off again,
A love-hate relationship.
Cora combed my hair in the mornings before I went to school,
Always having trouble finding the "part."
Cora said I should see about a part cut into my hair.
I told our barber, but he said that only coloreds did that, but he
Used a different word for coloreds.
I felt ashamed for having asked.
I remember people talking about the welfare system, especially food stamps.
They would say, you better get it before the coloreds do,
Only they, too, used other words.
Daddy drove a bread truck and kept his records in little
Receipt books with carbon papers.
I often played with his unused books,
Practicing my letters and words, and drawing my pictures.
Once I wrote the words "I love Cora" on the cover of one of the books.

Suddenly I remembered, I had to hurry and find that one book among a
    stack of books
That had been discarded outside in the trash,
Lest others read those words
And make fun of me for my feelings that I had dared to put in print.
As I grew older, I asked Daddy if I had to eat at the same table with Cora.
Daddy said it was okay to eat breakfast with Cora
If it were something light, like juice, toast, or cereal,
But lunch was different—I didn't have to eat lunch at the same table with
    her.
Cora came to work after Martin Luther King was assassinated.
The television shows reported the news and reactions both day and night.
We sat and wondered what the Blacks would do.
What would Cora do?
Daddy told Mother that if Cora said too much,
If she got too sassy,
Just give her money and send her home.
All Cora said was, "They killed our leader."
"They killed our leader."
Cora's face was sad but she uttered nothing more.
Her silence focused on sprinkling water from her soda bottle on the
    un-ironed laundry
Kept in the refrigerator for another ironing day's work.
We, too, kept silent.
One winter, Cora had the flu and couldn't work for about a week—
She had to be real sick to miss her three-dollar-a-day job.
Our family took her a big plate of food for her to eat.
Daddy didn't like the thought of her being cold, alone, and hungry.
Her wood-frame house moaned and creaked as we walked the bare floors.
Each room smelled with the aroma of burning kerosene and grease.
The wind could be felt inside her house.
She said "thank you" for the food.
Cora had spells in which she went to sleep upright with her head bowed,
Her head jerked up and then dropped down as she breathed noisily.
She must have been epileptic.
We were not to awaken her when she had one of her spells.
The spells always scared me—
What if she didn't wake up?

                                     

What was I supposed to do?
She could talk with a white cigarette, a Pall Mall, dangling from the corner
    of her mouth.
After sitting for a few minutes, watching morning television with us, she
    would
Say she had a lot of work ahead—dirty dishes, mopping floors, washing
    clothes,
Drying clothes on the line, ironing those clothes, and fixing food.
She had to "Shake, Rattle and Roll. Shake, Rattle and Roll."
She liked music and she liked to dance.
It came out in the newspaper from the Surgeon General that
Smoking could be hazardous to your health.
I told Cora not to smoke but she said
Her doctor offered her a cigarette while he smoked and examined her.
Cigarettes were thirty cents a pack.
Sometimes I would go to the store to buy them for her,
While she stayed home watching my younger brother and sister.
Once I went and handed the man twenty cents, two dimes, pulled from my
    front shirt pocket.
He said Cora knew they were thirty cents.
I told him that I was all I had, all the money Cora had given.
I retraced my steps with Cora, my brother and baby sister, until we came
    to the spot
Where I had bent over to tie laces of my tennis shoes.
Sure enough, in the dirt was the dime—it had fallen from my shirt pocket.
Cora got her smokes that day.
Cora sometimes talked about not having enough money.
I told Cora that she could save money by not smoking.
She told me that she had to live, too.
Cora had raised, rough scars on her arm—
Knife wounds, I would imagine.
Folks said that they liked to cut each other up on Saturday nights.
It was sometimes said with a laugh.
Once I climbed the apartment roof with some other kids.
I fell when I was trying to come down.
It knocked the wind out of me as I lay in the dirt and grass.
I looked up and the police were called—
I tried to crawl to Cora, whose arms were outstretched for me.

 

A neighborhood lady who was a nurse, she wouldn't let me move.
The nurse said I might have internal injuries.
I turned out all right.
Once it was raining hard, real hard as I went
Outside to ride the yellow school bus.
I was wearing Cora's see-through galoshes that she
Had given me to keep my feet dry.
Once Cora wanted to borrow some of my money;
I told her I would lend her the money if she signed a contract
With me in which, if she failed to repay the loan, I was entitled to repossess
    everything she owned.
She said it wouldn't be a real contract without a stamp.
The only stamps I knew about were postage stamps and Easter seals.
I told her that was okay with me, but she would have to buy the stamp.
I don't remember if I ever loaned her the money.
Cora came and went during those years.
I remember when Julia came on television—
It was the story of a Black widowed nurse and her little boy;
I think the little boy was named Corey.
I was always afraid my parents would catch me watching a show
About Black people.
What would they say?
We had race riots in my high school,
We had lock downs, the police were called—
It was not a pretty time.
There was a veteran substitute teacher on the day of the riot;
I remember her saying that she would substitute no more.
It wasn't worth it. It wasn't worth it.
When I went away to college,
My daddy said that if I had a Black roommate
At the state university, I would have to come home.
My roommate situation was okay; I didn't have to come home.
When I came home from college,
Cora would come to our house for a visit;
She always asked me to talk the college talk.
My mother would sometimes visit Cora
And eat in Cora's house,
Much to the surprise of my more prosperous aunt and uncle.

Cora died several months before my mother died,
My last living parent.
We began to dismantle the family household.
Had Cora been alive, we would have given her
The old washing machine and dryer.
Cora died before she would get the old washer and dryer.
Perhaps it was an unconscious token of what she had given us.
It was a world of separations—
Separate hospitals—one for whites and one for Blacks,
Different waiting rooms for coloreds and whites in the doctor's office.
Whites could go inside the Hash House to place their orders;
Coloreds had a separate outside window to place their orders.
Water fountains and bathrooms were separate,
Coloreds rode in the rear of the bus
And sat in the balcony of the local theatre.
It was seventh grade before I was in a class with a Black child;
Her name was Bernice.
Bernice was the only one in the English class who knew what an editorial
        was—
I suppose she had actually read them at home,
While we read the funny pages in black and white print.
An iron curtain existed in Europe; the Berlin wall would be constructed.
My sixth-grade teacher said that the Berlin wall would never fall.
There were other walls in that South, just as strong and just as deadly,
Keeping people locked into their places,
Sometimes in very heated and hated places.
I'm glad we no longer live in those places,
And that the Berlin wall would be broken by the people,
Sometimes slowly brick by brick and sometimes forcefully with
    sledgehammers.
I wish I could have liberated Cora but I had to be liberated first.
Memories remain, shameful memories of how we were
Before we knew any better.
Her memory and memories of the Berlin wall are still alive.
May our walls be broken, one by one.
When will full liberation come?

 

# Uninvited Guests

Birthday parties were common in the neighborhood where numerous children lived in the various lanes of the gated subdivision. The two brothers, new to the neighborhood, received the invitation from the young boy across the cul-de-sac. The invitation listed the customary information about the party, including the time—the traditional two hours in the evening. Excitedly, the two brothers arrived to the party with presents in hand.

Two hours later, the two boys returned home. While the older one quickly went to his room, the younger one lingered at the front door and looked at the house across the street. "Everything okay?" his mother asked.

The younger boy, with tears in his eyes, explained that the others at the party were staying there for a sleepover. He said, "I asked why couldn't I stay. He said he could only have five kids over for the sleepover. So we had to leave. Why did we have to leave, Mother? Why couldn't we stay?"

## Questions to Ponder

1. How can we promote benevolence and justice?
2. Were the two uninvited boys treated with kindness and justice?
3. Do we show preference in whom we treat with benevolence and justice?

# No Strings Attached

Kindness is one of the enduring characteristics that is traditionally associated with Christianity—though not always practiced by Christians. One of the first messages taught to preschoolers is typically "Be kind to one another." Those growing up in church life were taught the importance of showing kindness in gestures such as holding the door open for another person and saying, "Thank you." I remember in public school hearing the principal's intercom announcement about gathering shoes and clothes to help some needy children attend school. We collected shoes and clothes. In another annual emphasis, we collected dimes for the March of Dimes drive for the prevention of polio. How easily we became accustomed to participating in acts of benevolence and kindness.

I recall a member of the University Married Sunday School class that I taught as a college professor. After Sunday school was dismissed, he asked if he and his wife should accept monetary gifts from their generous and concerned parents.

"I know they want to be kind and helpful," stated the young man, yearning to be successfully independent, having married his girlfriend during their junior year. Once more he asked, "Should we accept those gifts?"

After my customary pause before speaking, I responded, "I do understand your wanting to be on your own and your parents and in-laws wanting to make life easier for you."

"Yeah," he gently said.

"I can't tell you to accept or to reject the offers," I said. "What I can say is to accept their gifts if that can make you grow to be independent and not dependent. Healthy adult gifts should come not to make us dependent but to aid us in growing to be independent."

"What would you say to our parents?" he asked.

"While your parents and in-laws have not asked me, I would say to them, 'Give to encourage independence. No strings attached.'"

"So it's a matter of how we would use it?" the young man asked.

Since this happened after Sunday school, I wish I had said, "You are close to the Kingdom." Instead, I smiled and nodded.

As an individual, as a church, or as a society, we are called to be kind in words, deeds, and justice. Our gifts or financial assistance to others should promote justice and fairness. True justice involves allowing all to experience opportunity. It's like the story of how giving an individual a fish feeds him for a day, while teaching him how to fish can help feed him for a lifetime. May justice flow naturally through both great and small acts. Let us expand our acts of kindness to provide justice and opportunity for all.

## Questions to Ponder

1. How important is it to show justice as we proclaim the Gospel?
2. Should benevolence be regarded as an aspect of justice?
3. What do you wish to happen when you give gifts to others?

# God of Kindness and Justice

God of kindness and justice, God of Jesus the Christ, God within each of us, we give thanks that you have not abandoned us today. Nor did you abandon our mothers and fathers of the past. We have lived in a world of darkness, a world of violence, a world of war, and a world of greed. Generations, both past and present, have contributed to these acts of unlove. Into this darkness, Jesus, the Son of God, was born and led a life for each of us. This Spirit made flesh has changed darkness into light, violence into harmony, war into peace, and greed into benevolence.

Help us to be the kindness and justice that was born in the darkness of human need and rebellion, love that was exposed to criticism and misunderstanding, and love that was offered to all who might believe. Renew within us the freshness of belief and the maturity of understanding of our belief. Transform us in these day as we seek to be your instruments of individual and social transformation. We pause, we prepare, and we practice for the coming of the Kingdom in fuller measures of justice and kindness. In the name of Jesus the Crucified, we pray. Amen.

# TIMES OF BIBLICAL EMPHASIS

*So then faith cometh by hearing, and hearing by the word of God.*
—Romans 10:17

*The Bible is the cradle wherein Christ is laid.*
—Martin Luther

*It is time that Christians were judged more by their likeness to Christ than notions of Christ.*
—Lucretia Mott

No one item has had more influence on the Christian movement than the Bible—carefully preserved from precious oral traditions into written records, passed from one generation to the next. Scholars agree that the words found in Scripture began in oral form before being recorded in written form. The Babylonian captivity allowed for the children of Abraham to gather their Scriptures to convey God's truth to future generations in what we now know as the Old Testament. In the New Testament are the Pauline letters, some of which were circulated among various early churches. Other important letters were recorded and circulated to those churches. The written Gospels appeared after the Pauline letters. Scholars generally agree that these records were written years after the actual events portrayed in them. The formalization of the Bible as we know it today was a process over hundreds of years.

Once formulated and recognized, the Bible provided a common call for unity to those who could read and those who heard it read. Organizational hierarchy and power developed in the maturing church. Soon, interpretation of what the words meant came into question. Battles, through debate and through physical warfare, ensued. Challenges and challengers to traditional interpretation were eliminated. New faith traditions and later denominations emerged. Lives were lost in the defense of the traditional faith and in the fight for individual rights of interpretation.

Even in the twenty-first century, struggles surround the Bible. Much of the fight and its ensuing division concerns the interpretation of specific passages such as creation, the role of men and women, topics of leadership, topics of marriage, and the beginning of human life. Often individuals are hesitant to consider new understandings of the Bible because it may conflict with other interpretations they have heard from beloved pastors, teachers, or family members. New understandings create dilemmas of learning and loyalty. People in diverse types of exile, however, may have a unique opportunity for biblical renewal and understanding.

Congregations benefit from being educated about how to read, study, interpret, and be guided by the Bible. Not only should the content be taught, but also the congregation should be taught how to approach Bible study in an honest and consistent fashion. Loving the Bible does not mean that we must abandon the best scholarly understandings of the Bible.

 

Elevate the importance of the Bible as you provide sound and challenging biblical exposition. Gently and enthusiastically teach biblical relevance from the cradle to the maturing years. Relational credibility, built through years of trusted ministry, aids in the growing acceptance of new biblical insights and applications.

The following pages provide supplemental resources that might enhance the importance of biblical emphasis. You will find several hymns, readings, stories and theological reflections, and a seasonal prayer. May these resources become a seasoning to add new flavor to proper emphasis on the Bible. May you experience new imaginations, insights, and actions.

# Come, Holy Spirit, Lord

**Claude Douglas Bryan**

**Suggested Tune: BETHANY**
**Meter: 6.4.6.4.6.6.6.4.**

Come, Holy Spirit, Lord,
Through Holy Word.
Now open hearts and minds
Through spoken Word.
The Holy Word, a gift,
That brings a life of faith—
To follow Christ the Son.
Thy Word gives life!

Give eyes so we might see
The message clear—
How we might live on earth
With peace and love.
How blest we are this day,
The studied Word so near
Becomes new Living Word
To guide our lives.

Keep still what would distract
Our hearts from thee.
May lives be shaped today
Through Scriptures clear.
Inspire to service true,
To seek thy will to do,
To find the face of God
Through Living Word.

# Keep Us Open

**Claude Douglas Bryan**

**Suggested Tune: BEACH SPRING**
**Meter: 8.7.8.7.D.**

Keep us open to thy Scripture, where lives broken might be changed.
Glide us forward in this wonder—heart no longer found estranged.
Keep us open to thy mercy, where forgiveness we would find.
Guide through words and deeds of kindness—making hopes and dreams
 refined.

Keep us open to thy power, where the weak might be made strong.
Give directions for thy purpose—seeking change for what is wrong.
Keep us open to thy presence, where our sight might be made clear.
Grant us wisdom as we follow—loving all whom God holds dear.

Keep us open to these moments, where young lives and texts shall meet.
Give us guidance in our teaching—may new truths we always greet.
Keep us open to new ventures, where we join with heart and mind.
Grant renewal in our spirit, leaving only love behind.

Keep us open to thy calling, where both young and old shall meet.
Grow us faithful in this mission—till our work on earth's complete.
Keep us open to thy future, where thy church shall be reformed;
Grace us inward through our journey—knowing Christ we are transformed.

# Holy Scripture, Books of Wonder (Poem)

Holy Scripture, Books of Wonder,
Records of the Holy One,
and the human creation.
Struggling to know and to be known,
Moments of running and hiding,
Stories of praise and sorrow,
Captured and raptured,
Stories caught on sacred page.
Ordinary becoming extraordinary,
Imperfect lenses and imperfect pens,
Imperfect discovering the Perfect.
One generation to the next,
Ongoing battles of meaning,
Holy Scripture, Books of Wonder.

## Questions to Ponder

1. How would you describe the Bible to another person in ways that would communicate meaning?
2. What is the role of humans in the Bible?
3. What, if any, struggles do you experience with the Bible?

# Guide Us, O Lord (Responsive Reading)

LEADER: Guide us, O Lord, as we seek to study Scripture so that we might increase in believing and understanding.

**PEOPLE:** Guide us, O Lord.

LEADER: Guide us, O Lord, as we seek to understand the sacred pages of Scripture that reveal to us the love God has for Creation.

**PEOPLE:** Guide us, O Lord.

LEADER: Guide us, O Lord. May the Holy Spirit that inspired instruct us into fuller understanding and appreciation for your Word.

**PEOPLE:** Guide us, O Lord.

LEADER: Guide us, O Lord, as we seek to study so that we will be found pleasing to you.

**PEOPLE:** Guide us, O Lord.

LEADER: Guide us, O Lord, as we proclaim your majesty to all the world, serving all with equality and generosity.

**PEOPLE:** Guide us, O Lord.

LEADER: Guide us, O Lord, as we seek to be transformed anew into your image as revealed through Jesus the Christ.

**PEOPLE:** Guide us, O Lord.

*ALL:* Guide us, O Lord, as we seek to be transformed anew into your image as revealed through Jesus the Christ. Amen.

# First-Year Bible

The young man carried a big red Bible as a nineteen-year-old. He continued to carry the same Bible forty-five years later. Purchased new, the book began its life as a student Bible in the man's first and only undergraduate Bible class. Its binding is worn, frayed. It has underlined words, phrases, and entire verses. Sometimes there are arrows drawn on its passages. His inscriptions, "see also," guide him to other portions of Scripture.

He has other Bibles that are newer, more beautiful, better translations. When asked why he carries this old red Bible, he replied that this Bible reminds him of his first religion teacher who introduced him to a scholarly approach to the study of the Old and New Testaments. It reminds him of what his teacher faced every year.

Each semester as the teacher entered the classroom, he confronted a wide range of minds, some open, some closed, some with all the answers, some with no questions, and some with many questions and no answers. Each semester he had to address students who questioned his basic Christian discipleship because the teacher proposed probing questions and used a vocabulary of unfamiliar technical terms. Each year he faced students who doubted his Christian experience. One of the teacher's goals was to expand biblical inquiry, to explain and not explain away.

Carrying the Bible was a tribute to this teacher and to others who teach faithfully even when they might be misunderstood and not appreciated.

## Questions to Ponder

1. How would you describe the Bible?
2. How does the Bible enter your everyday life?
3. How can we maintain both the mystery and a deeper understanding of the Bible?

 

# Yellow Bread Truck

His father drove a yellow bread truck for a living. Rising at three a.m., six days a week, the father rode up and down the major highways and country roads, delivering bread to large grocery chains and to small mom-and-pop stores. Getting home around five p.m., the exhausted man would park his bread truck near his apartment. On Sundays, he would sleep most of the day; he could sleep as much as he wanted. The family did not attend church.

One evening on the back bumper of the bread truck, two neighborhood boys who went to church coached the bread deliveryman's younger son. The bumper became a preaching or teaching platform. Here the young boy first heard the message of evangelism. The two brothers took delight at teaching the young, unchurched boy to recite John 3:16. Their names were Eddie and Paul. These young child evangelists unknown to anyone else were the first ones to bring the boy the verbal message of Jesus. The recipient of their witness would become a university teacher and active churchman. The words of children playing were remembered as the first ones to teach him about God's love for all of creation, including himself.

He would go on to learn more about the Bread of Life. The two boys would precede him in death. One would die in his late teens and the other in his sixties. They and their families never knew the role they played in bringing the Bread of Life to the young boy on the rear bumper of an ordinary bread truck.

## Questions to Ponder

1. How much knowledge is needed to teach the gospel to others?
2. Can a slice of bread become a whole loaf of bread?
3. How is the Bread of Life communicated?

# Warning: Learning Ahead

A church study discussion on the nature of the Bible was going in circles of misunderstanding and emerging inhospitality and suspicion. Those who were well-seasoned Bible teachers, many of them seminary or university graduates, were judicious in what they said. In contrast, those present who knew less were more emphatic in their proclamations and understandings. The words of interpretation were not well received by those who wanted more definitive answers. Two young married couples were overtly disturbed.

A frustrated young couple declared, "We want to know what the Bible says and not just opinions on what it says."

I knew we were in deep trouble and not ready for discussion of issues relating to topics inherent in the couple's statements, such as phenomenology and epistemology. How do you respond in words that are honest and on topic? Finally, I broke my silence.

"I wish I could give you simple answers. Personally, I do not study and teach the Bible literally. I study and teach the Bible seriously in hopes of understanding its message of the past and its words to the present."

Several other adults reinforced what I said. From overhearing snippets of after-class discussion, I knew my contribution was not universally appreciated. One of the couples had been reared in the church from the cradle to this moment; the other couple had minimal church contact.

We study it each week in Sunday school and in other teaching sessions; we read it and hear it spoken each Sunday from the pulpit; and we hear its messages proclaimed. As you have guessed, it is the Bible, vital to the life and mission of the church. Tragically, too many lifelong church members are uninformed about the nature of the Bible.

Too many church members have not learned how to read the Bible. They have been exposed to what I would call a poor pathology of the Bible. They have heard the Bible dissected into small, unrelated parts in Sunday school and in sermons, much like a pathology approach that would take only one sample to make broad generalizations and pronouncements. Good pathology involves multiple samples and slides for examination and study. Poor pathology leads to poor Bible understanding. It does not consider the various literary forms found in the Bible, the intention of the writer and text, and the needs and characteristics of the original audience.

While reading may seem quite simple, it is very complex. Reading is an exhausting privilege often taken for granted. Even in the study of the Bible, we may fail to understand its literary nature with such elements as time, location, authorship, literary style, historical basis, and language. Producing biblically literate congregations is not easy or quick. But failing to engage in this quest for reading and studying the Bible is perennial. Without this level of study, we fail to cultivate an environment of discriminating minds and willing hearts to receive the Word of God.

## Questions to Ponder

1. How would you communicate your understanding of the Bible to believers? To nonbelievers?
2. How do you maintain harmony and cooperation in congregations that are divided in their opinions on the Bible?
3. "Read and believe." How do you respond to those three words?

## God of the Matriarchs and the Patriarchs

God of the Matriarchs and the Patriarchs, God revealed in Jesus the Crucified, we share these moments of gratitude for the wonderful ways you have spoken to us in the past, speak to us in the present, and will speak to us in the future. We are grateful for the precious witness recorded in Holy Scripture.

Within its pages, we find portraits of you as you interact with human creation. You are within us in our moments of delight, moments of despair, moments of loneliness, moments of grief, moments of bounty, and moments of hunger. The stories and declaration recorded in the Bible give us pause to be in awe of the magnitude of your love for humankind. Your word reveals to us our broken human condition and the hope that you offer each of us in our healing.

Give us the patience to read this Record with seriousness, anticipation, and joy. Surprise us as we find meanings, both old and new, within its pages. May we seek Scripture's witness of who we are; what we might be; and how we should treat both familiar and unfamiliar faces. May this Word become a Living Word that grows within us in the coming years. Increase our understanding so we might increase devotion to you and to others. Give us peace in this time and place. May we not stray from this wonderful testimony of life with you. In the name of Jesus the Crucified, we pray. Amen.

# TIMES OF CREATION CELEBRATIONS

*The heavens declare the glory of God;*
*and the firmament sheweth his handywork.*
—Psalm 19:1

*Thou hast created us for Thyself,*
*and our heart is not quiet until it rests in Thee.*
—St. Augustine

*All my relations in creation.*
—Cherokee Proverb

By his actions he regarded the world as a large garden composed of many smaller gardens. Sometimes apples, roses, blueberries, or tomatoes. His name was Jack. Jack was a multitalented individual. He was born in central Texas to a Baptist family, married, had a family, served as a Baptist missionary in East Africa, and taught at a Baptist-affiliated university in North Carolina.

I first met Jack when he was completing his doctoral work while on furlough. He taught me the first half of the Old Testament. I met Jack again years later as I assumed a teaching post at the university where he had recently retired. He was skilled in Swahili as well as in understanding the biblical languages. He could preach, teach, debate, and haul manure with the best of them. Whatever game he played, he played to win.

Jack was a gardener, both in Africa and in North Carolina. He had learned to cultivate apple-producing trees in a region thought too elevated to grow apples. In North Carolina, he was known for both his flowers and his tomatoes. Wherever one might find oneself, in familiar and unfamiliar places, Jack believed that each person needed to work in a garden.

This scholar of the Old Testament lived where the first story of human creation was told. He lived in a garden. He tilled it and shared his produce with friends and church family. He saw the importance of staying close to nature. The scholar-teacher-missionary tended the university rose garden. After his death, the garden pavilion was named for him.

One of his favorite Old Testament prophets was Amos, a farmer from Tekoa. The message of Amos described Jack: "to love mercy and to walk humbly with your God" (Micah 6:8).

As a member of Jack's Sunday school class, the Kerygma (Greek word for proclamation) Class, I witnessed Jack's communication with class members and other interested individuals through email. He ended his messages with the phrase "In the Fellowship"—a simple phrase but a powerful one if uttered by Jack.

Jack was an individual who took the phrase and the commitment very seriously. Whether he was in the fellowship of Rotary, the fellowship of the university, the fellowship of his local church, or the fellowship of a rose garden, Jack gave himself wholeheartedly.

 

There is something mystical, spiritual, and even healing about tending a garden. From a small seed or a small investment new life emerges. Understanding our world as a garden requires our becoming a gardener. The creation story describes humankind as established within a garden. Humans were instructed to tend the garden and to tend our brothers and sisters. We celebrate creation and honor God when we nurture creation and nurture one another.

The following pages provide supplemental resources that might enhance the preparation for celebrating creation. You will find several hymns, readings, stories and theological reflections, and a seasonal prayer. May these resources become a seasoning to add new flavor to this important celebration. May you experience new imaginations, insights, and actions.

# God Is the Great I Am

**Claude Douglas Bryan**

**Suggested Tune: TERRA PATRIS**
**Meter: 6.6.8.6.D.**

God is the Great I am
Whose Word began all life;
So carefully and joyfully,
This world God shares with us;
God is the Great I am;
We find our life in him;
From pain and tears, Christ brings us hope
To guide the days we live.

God is the Great I am
Who loves us where we are;
Our doubts and fears to Christ we bring
For healing from his touch;
God is the Great I am;
No one can steal this joy
That lives from Christ's atoning grace
In all who would believe.

God is the Great I am
Who comforts us in grief;
Our deepest sorrows God will bless
And help us find our rest.
God is the Great I am
Who seeks to find the lost
To bring them back to heaven's home
For all eternity.

God is the Great I am
Through Christ, we can find life;
In Him, we find God's gifts for us
As children of the King.
God is the Great I am
Who speaks to us today;
We share the message of this Love
Across eternity.

# Lord of Creation

**Claude Douglas Bryan**

**Suggested Tune: SLANE**
**Meter: 10.10.10.10.**

Lord of creation, by him life first breathed;
Jesus was born and earth he did serve;
Love shown though living and dying for all;
Placing our lives in faith, trusting his word alone.

Faith in Jesus brings salvation this day;
This, too, a gift from his heaven above;
Not by merit but God's grace alone;
Dwelling, transforming all broken anew.

Worldly concerns would divert thoughts from you;
Evil surrounds and distracts us from peace,
Daily we need your renewal and care,
More like the Savior who lives in this place.

Lord, we still need your salvation today;
Save us from robbers of your tender care;
Pour out your Spirit, like David of old,
Breathing your life in us, guarding us through these days.

# Lump of Clay I (Poem)

On the days of wondrous creation,
Mysteries beyond explanation,
God spoke turning darkness into light.
Love's handiwork was good within his sight.

God took a lump of clay
From earth one special day,
Giving new life and play
Into a lump of clay.

The earth and her creatures were God's masterpiece,
Yet humans would be would the centerpiece.
God reached down and scooped from the depth of earth.
By his love and his breath, we found our birth.

God took a lump of clay
From earth one special day,
Giving new life and play
Into a lump of clay.

## Questions to Ponder

1. What meaning does the phrase "lump of clay" suggest about our human nature?
2. What meaning does the phrase "lump of clay" suggest about God's nature?
3. What is the role of humans in the created order?
4. How well have humans contributed harmony and wholeness to God's creation?

 

# Creation Narrative (Choral Reading)

## Genesis 1:1-31; 2:1-3

*Note: You may wish to have soft music playing in the background.*

LEADER 1: [1:1] In the beginning God created the heaven and the earth. [2] And the earth was without form, and void; and darkness was upon the face of the deep. And the Spirit of God moved upon the face of the waters.

*CHOIR:* God began.

**ALL:** Praise to God.

LEADER 2: [3] And God said, Let there be light: and there was light. [4] And God saw the light, that it was good: and God divided the light from the darkness. [5] And God called the light Day, and the darkness he called Night. And the evening and the morning were the first day.

*CHOIR:* God began. God called.

**ALL:** Praise to God.

LEADER 3: [6] And God said, Let there be a firmament in the midst of the waters, and let it divide the waters from the waters. [7] And God made the firmament, and divided the waters which were under the firmament from the waters which were above the firmament: and it was so. [8] And God called the firmament Heaven. And the evening and the morning were the second day.

*CHOIR:* God began. God called. God made.

**ALL:** Praise to God.

LEADER 1: [9] And God said, Let the waters under the heaven be gathered together unto one place, and let the dry land appear: and it was so. [10] And God called the dry land Earth; and the gathering together of the waters called he Seas: and God saw that it was good.

*CHOIR:* God began. God called. God made. God saw.

**ALL:** Praise to God

LEADER 2: [11] And God said, Let the earth bring forth grass, the herb yielding seed, and the fruit tree yielding fruit after his kind, whose seed is in itself, upon the earth: and it was so. [12] And the earth brought forth grass, and herb yielding seed after his kind, and the tree yielding fruit, whose seed was, after his kind: and God saw that it was good. [13] And the evening and the morning were the third day.

*CHOIR:* God began. God called. God made. God saw.

**ALL:** Praise to God.

LEADER 3: [14] And God said, Let there be lights in the firmament of the heaven to divide the day from the night; and let them be for signs, and for times, and for days, and years: [15] And let them be for lights in the firmament of the heaven to give light upon the earth: and it was so. [16] And God made two great lights; the greater light to rule the day, and the lesser light to rule the night: he made the stars also. [17] And God set them in the firmament of the heaven to give light upon the earth, [18] And to rule over the day and over the night, and to divide the light from the darkness: and God saw that it was good. [19] And the evening and the morning were the fourth day.

*CHOIR:* God began. God called. God made. God saw. God set.

**ALL:** Praise to God.

LEADER 1: [20] And God said, Let the waters bring forth abundantly the moving creature that hath life, and fowl that may fly above the earth in the open firmament of heaven. [21] And God created great whales, and every living creature that moveth, which the waters brought forth abundantly, after their kind, and every winged fowl after his kind: and God saw that it was good. [22] And God blessed them, saying, Be fruitful, and multiply, and fill the waters in the seas, and let fowl multiply in the earth. [23] And the evening and the morning were the fifth day.

*CHOIR:* God began. God called. God made. God saw. God set. God blessed.

 

**ALL:** Praise to God.

LEADER 2: [24] And God said, Let the earth bring forth the living creature after his kind, cattle, and creeping thing, and beast of the earth after his kind: and it was so. [25] And God made the beast of the earth after his kind, and cattle after their kind, and every thing that creepeth upon the earth after his kind: and God saw that it was good.

*CHOIR:* God began. God called. God made. God saw. God set. God blessed.

**ALL:** Praise to God.

LEADER 3: [26] And God said, Let us make man in our image, after our likeness: and let them have dominion over the fish of the sea, and over the fowl of the air, and over the cattle, and over all the earth, and over every creeping thing that creepeth upon the earth.

*CHOIR:* God began. God called. God made. God saw. God set. God blessed.

**ALL:** Praise to God.

LEADER 1: [27] So God created man in his own image, in the image of God created he him; male and female created he them.

*CHOIR:* God began. God called. God made. God saw. God set. God blessed. God created.

**ALL:** Praise to God.

LEADER 2: [28] And God blessed them, and God said unto them, Be fruitful, and multiply, and replenish the earth, and subdue it: and have dominion over the fish of the sea, and over the fowl of the air, and over every living thing that moveth upon the earth.

*CHOIR:* God began. God called. God made. God saw. God set. God blessed. God created.

**ALL:** Praise to God.

LEADER 3: [29] And God said, Behold, I have given you every herb bearing seed, which is upon the face of all the earth, and every tree, in the which is the fruit of a tree yielding seed; to you it shall be for meat. [30] And to every beast of the earth, and to every fowl of the air, and to every thing that creepeth upon the earth, wherein there is life, I have given every green herb for meat: and it was so.

*CHOIR:* God began. God called. God made. God saw. God set. God blessed. God created. God gave.

**ALL:** Praise to God.

LEADER 1: [31] And God saw every thing that he had made, and, behold, it was very good. And the evening and the morning were the sixth day.

*CHOIR:* God began. God called. God made. God saw. God set. God blessed. God created. God gave.

LEADER 2: [2:1] Thus the heavens and the earth were finished, and all the host of them. [2] And on the seventh day God ended his work which he had made; and he rested on the seventh day from all his work which he had made.

*CHOIR:* God began. God called. God made. God saw. God set. God blessed. God created. God gave. God ended. God rested.

**ALL:** Praise to God.

LEADER 3: [3] And God blessed the seventh day, and sanctified it: because that in it he had rested from all his work which God created and made.

*CHOIR:* God began. God called. God made. God saw. God set. God blessed. God created. God gave. God ended. God rested. God sanctified.

**ALL:** Praise to God.

LEADER 1: In the beginning...

**ALL:** God. God said it was very good. Praise to God. Amen.

 

# Aunt Minnie's Mimosa Tree

The family was experiencing their traditional summer visit from Aunt Minnie. Aunt Minnie was in her seventies. Having reared her family through the years before and after World War II, she had known both prosperity and depression. Aunt Minnie helped raise her nephew, the child of her sister, after his mother died. Having only daughters, she loved her nephew as a son and sought to provide motherly love and guidance.

With the sun in her eyes, Aunt Minnie sat with her nephew's children in the backyard. "We need some shade. Help me up," she said. "We've got a hole to dig and then we're going to the woods."

Aunt Minnie and the three children went into the woods, where she spotted a young mimosa sapling. "Dig here," she said, "but be careful that you get the tap root. That's real important. Even humans need tap roots." When questioned about digging in someone else's woods, Aunt Minnie said, "God owns the earth. I'm simply redistributing his creation."

After a successful dig and filling in the hole, Aunt Minnie marched the three children with the newly acquired mimosa back to their home. She directed the relocating of the mimosa into its newly dug hole, showing the children how to pack around it with the amended soil. Aunt Minnie said, "You must water this every day for six weeks. Let's mark it on the calendar."

Following her directions, the children watched the tree grow. Next summer came and Minnie found the tree alive and well. "I bet in a few years we can sit under it."

True to her prediction, in the fourth summer the mimosa provided some shade. The mimosa continued to grow year by year, even when Aunt Minnie's visits stopped. In the ensuing years, the mimosa was trimmed back to what was thought to be death. But much to the surprise of everyone, the mimosa tree came back year after year.

## Questions to Ponder

1. What value do you think Aunt Minnie was trying to teach the children?
2. What qualities promote creation's resilience?
3. What do you do to promote resilience in yourself and others?
4. Was Aunt Minnie right about humans needing tap roots? Explain.
5. How can we promote tap roots for those in the Christian community?

# Creation Upkeep

To the best of my knowledge, my family had been farmers over seventy-five years ago when they left farming for the textile mills. Although not a farmer, my mother always planted tomatoes. It was often an unspoken competition between her and my paternal uncle. Who would have the first tomato of the season? My mother or my uncle? I did not inherit any type of horticulture gene.

While I love a beautiful lawn, I do not enjoy making that beauty possible. I have vision for what should be, but lack energy and commitment to achieve it. Proverbs 29:18 states, "where there is no vision, the people perish." Where there is no vision and work, the plants and lawn also perish.

After the initial plantings, my advice to the plants is to follow the adage "root hog or die." In my mind, the plants are on their own. Best wishes. Fortunately, my wife engages in much of the creative maintenance of the yard. I am not a master gardener by anyone's standards. While I enjoy the results, I do not enjoy the moments leading to them.

Success in gardens and landscapes involves tending to the soil. Selecting the right plants and complementary plants, timing the plantings, locating optimal sunshine and drainage, tilling the soil, amending the soil as needed, determining the best depth of planting, spacing the plants, and maintaining faithful waterings are elements of the overall process. Appreciation of creation involves an understanding of what goes into its blooming maturity.

Among the recorded teachings of Jesus are numerous agrarian metaphors, often describing the Kingdom of God and the disciple's life. Lessons appropriate to life can easily be gained from agriculture. Whether it be for beauty or nourishment, work is necessary. Creation needs our involvement; we need to be involved in creation. We can bring out the best in gardens; gardens can bring out the best in us.

## Questions to Ponder

1. How important is it to be involved in creation? Explain.
2. What can be learned from gardening?
3. What can we learn about ourselves and life from creation? Explain.
4. How are you involved in the maintenance and flourishing of creation?
5. What are the elements of nourishing the Christian life? Explain.

 

## Master Creator and Loving Sustainer

Master Creator and Loving Sustainer, you called all things into being by the power of your voice. As you commanded, it was so. We are grateful that in your providence you created us, spread throughout the world with different languages and customs. Yet in this creation, we are called to be one though we in truth are many. Whether it be the smallness of potted plants or the great rainforests, you created life; from a trinkle of water from a faucet to mighty rivers and waterfalls, you created life. From the great world of Olympians to those impaired with illness and disease, you created; from the great minds of the scientific laboratories to a baby beginning to make first sounds, you created; from the high courts of law to family discussions, you created; and from the world of art to the small pieces of paper with a child's scribbles, you are a part of all of this. Help us, O Creator, to value all of life and its creations, as they are gifts from you.

Help us to find ways we might partner with you in both creating and sustaining your creation. As the best stewards, may our actions reflect genuine compassion and reverence. Thank you for those moments when we stand or sit in awe of all you have done. Help us to learn to sow, to water, to prune, to value, and to nurture these wonderful gifts. May your spirit find a welcome in all the deepest places of our hearts so we might learn to love your creation. May we enjoy creation, always remembering it is not ours alone. In the name of Jesus the Crucified, we pray. Amen.

# TIMES OF DEATH AND GRIEF

*And God shall wipe away all tears from their eyes; and there shall be no more death, neither sorrow, nor crying, neither shall there be any more pain: for the former things are passed away.*
—Revelation 21:4

*When your time comes to die, be not like those whose hearts are filled with fear of death, so that when their time comes they weep and pray for a little more time to live their lives over again in a different way. Sing your death song, and die like a hero going home.*
—Tecumseh

*God washes her eyes by tears until they can behold the invisible land where tears shall come no more.*
—Harriet Beecher Stowe

I became aware of death early in life. I have a vague recollection of my maternal great-grandmother's death. I remember her erratic eating habits, eating with her fingers. When I questioned her behavior with my grandmother, my grandmother said her mother was in her "second childhood." Later, death would become more familiar when I was twelve or so with the passing of my maternal grandmother and grandfather. My paternal grandparents had died before I was born. Later, an aunt would die when I was around fourteen years of age. At nineteen I watched my father die following a year of heart-related struggles. Death was no stranger and has become more familiar with the passing of the years.

Explorations of death are common themes in literature. In my sophomore year, I read of David Copperfield, who was born after the death of his father and thrust into an unfriendly world following the death of his mother. In an American literature survey course, I studied William Cullen Bryant's "Thanatopsis," a view of death. Cullen describes death as a "moving caravan." Later I would read of Freud's idea that the goal of all life was to die. In sociology I read the pioneer work of Elisabeth Kübler-Ross on the stages of death. Both personal experience and educational settings introduced me to death.

We cannot escape death and its impact on family, friends, and church. Coping skills and faith are vital. As a caring community, we need to find meaningful ways to support those experiencing death and grief. We must appropriately acknowledge what we cannot escape, only delay. Accepting the inevitability of death can enhance our living intentionally. What is it that we must accomplish before death and resurrection? The Christian faith holds many answers.

The following pages provide supplemental resources that might enhance the preparation for the observation of death and grieving. You will find several hymns, readings, stories and theological reflections, and a seasonal prayer. May these resources become a seasoning to add new flavor to this important observation. May you experience new imaginations, insights, and actions.

# A Kerygma (Proclamation) Gift

**Claude Douglas Bryan**              **Suggested Tunes: TALLIS CANON**
**MARYTON**
**Meter: 8.8.8.8.**

God spoke the Word, our world was born;
Rebellion caused the earth to mourn;
From Eden's gates, our plight began—
Both life and death, our caravan.

A special art belongs to each,
Such treasures both to live and teach,
Bestowed from God's own loving heart—
This love for others to impart.

Our hearts are weary for our loss;
Eternal life through Calvary's cross,
Redemption claims the ones reborn;
Their earthly absence we shall mourn.

The ones we love from us depart;
Farewells, though brief, leave broken hearts.
Their joy and laughter still will chime;
We understand not heaven's time.

On earth we live but for a day;
This loved one's life showed us the way.
From tasks divine may we not stray;
This faith and love we shall convey.

Thy grace gives hope that will sustain,
Until we move beyond earth's plane,
With calming peace more than suffice,
To open gates in Paradise.

Remind us, Lord, we live and die,
Though never from thy watchful eye;
Our Lord who walked the world we knew
Will greet us when our journey's through.

# When Days of Sadness

**Claude Douglas Bryan**

**Suggested Tune: ST.COLUMBIA**

**Meter: 8.7.8.7.**

When days of sadness fill our lives, great loss and sorrow know;
Unanswered questions plague our minds; O Lord, please answer why.

When pains of parting we must bear; when loved ones move from touch;
To thee we come with broken heart; reshape our shattered lives.

When shock gives way to disbelief, returning doubts and fears
As anger comes and blame persists, help each avoid despair.

Renew us now, we pray, O Lord, please strengthen lives within;
Support through love another's hurt, the comfort thou bestows.

# O Lord, We Gather in This Place

**Claude Douglas Bryan**

**Suggested Tunes: AVON
CRIMOND
MAITLAND
ST. ANNE
ST. PETER
Meter: 8.6.8.6.**

O Lord, we gather in this place
To share our fond farewell
For one we love who ran the race
And now with thee does dwell.

How blest are we for we have known
God's fellowship of love.
On earth our loved ones are on loan
Till called to life above.

Shared memories shall not be lost
In this is comfort sure;
Thy own dear Son fulfilled the cost
That brings us hope secure.

Now, Lord, grant peace that stills our grief
In Jesus' name we pray;
We praise our God for this belief
In our reunion day.

 

# A Watch to Keep

**Claude Douglas Bryan**

**Suggested Tunes: SWEET HOUR**
**HE LEADETH ME**
**Meter: 8.8.8.8.D.**

When I must leave my earthly
  home,
My spirit shall no longer roam;
All pain and sadness left behind,
Sweet memories are only mine;
Be mindful of the place I go;
This comfort would I have you
  know
That when on earth your time is
  done,
There will I wait for you to come.

When I no longer pass the plate
Or visit at the neighbor's gate;
When I no longer say Amen
Or join in fellowship again,
Be mindful of the place I go;
This comfort would I have you
  know
That when on earth your time is
  done,
There will I wait for you to come.

When I no longer eat the bread,
I shall have nothing more to dread;
The price was paid for you and me,
Forgiveness found at Calvary;
Be mindful of the place I go;
This comfort would I have you
  know
That when on earth your time is
  done,
There will I wait for you to come.

From God, we have a watch to
  keep,
To love and feed his little sheep;
In death and life, from place to
  place,
God guides all those who claim his
  grace;
Be mindful of the place I go;
This comfort would I have you
  know
That when on earth your time is
  done,
There will I wait for you to come.

# Showing Up (Poem)

What do you say
To one who is grieving?
The words escape me.
How can I reach them?
Am I supposed to have the answers?
How to make sense out of nonsense?

Listening is what you do;
Listening with your ears clear,
Your eyes focused and unwavering;
Putting away distracting thoughts and excursions;
Listening for what is said and not said;
Looking at what is done and not done.

Hearing the same questions repeated,
Not judging but only listening.
Reflecting thoughts and feelings,
Embrace without anxiety the silence;
Let their pace be your guide, only
Showing up, Showing up.

## Questions to Ponder

1. What do you think is the struggle for the writer of the poem?
2. What practical instructions does the author propose for listening?
3. What is the most important part of the process of being with someone in grief or loss?

## For Those Who Mourn (Responsive Reading)

LEADER: Our heavenly Father, you are the creator and sustainer of your creation. No part of your creation is beyond your love and power. We ask your presence, your comfort, your guidance, and your protection this day. Our heavenly Creator, we come here today to share in community in the passing of ________________. You instruct that "blessed are those that mourn, for they shall be comforted" (Matthew 5:4). Jesus said, "Let not your heart be troubled: ye believe in God,  believe also in me" (John 14:1).

**PEOPLE:** "God is our refuge and strength, a very present help in trouble" (Psalm 46:1).

LEADER: Our Father, we do not understand the "whys" of death. Our minds cannot make sense out of what appears to be nonsense. Your Scripture says, "My flesh and my heart faileth: but God is the strength of my heart, and my portion forever" (Psalm 73:26).

**PEOPLE:** "God is our refuge and strength, a very present help in trouble" (Psalm 46:1).

LEADER: We know we can bring our grief, our sadness, and our questions to you. "The LORD is nigh unto them that are of a broken heart; and saveth such as be of a contrite spirit" (Psalm 34:18).

**PEOPLE:** "God is our refuge and strength, a very present help in trouble" (Psalm 46:1).

LEADER: Give us abiding comfort in these moments and in the days ahead as we seek to find life without our loved one. Console us with your word and your spirit. "The LORD thy God in the midst of thee is mighty; he will save; he will rejoice over thee with joy; he will rest in his love, he will joy over thee with singing" (Zephaniah 3:17). "But I will sing of thy power; yea, I will sing aloud of thy mercy in the morning: for thou has been my defence and refuge in the day of my trouble" (Psalm 59:16).

**PEOPLE:** "God is our refuge and strength, a very present help in trouble" (Psalm 46:1).

LEADER: "The last enemy that shall be destroyed is death" (1 Corinthians 15:26).

*ALL:* "God is our refuge and strength, a very present help in trouble" (Psalm 46:1).

# Line 'em Up

A group of mothers, some young and others older, invited the wise women of their neighborhood group to join them for coffee and cookies. These mothers often asked older women for advice about family, especially their children. One woman had recently experienced the loss of both her parents, her children's beloved and involved grandparents. The grieving woman, her voice broken by tears and hesitations, asked, "How can we teach our children not to fear death?" The room was silent.

One wise woman said, "I'm not sure if this will help, but let me say, before we teach our children, we must face our own fears. Let me share with you what I have learned." The woman began to describe her views.

"Death is like an extensive line of people who are standing in line to meet loved ones who have gone through a door. Generally, the older ones are closer to the head of the line and younger ones are at the rear of the line. Within this moving line, some people are standing strong, some are stooped over, and unexpectedly some people suddenly break in line. Sometimes young ones move to the front of the line. We may ask questions on why, but we will not find satisfying answers."

Facial expressions were fixed on the woman who spoke.

"My faith has helped me face death and grief. Sometimes there is peace; sometimes there is anguish. But we are all moving forward. It is part of the natural human process. We leave one community for another community. We cannot avoid the line or our place in the line. We can learn from others as they find peace within their part of the journey."

## Questions to Ponder

1. What is the value, if any, of describing death as an extensive line of people?
2. Why do some individuals break in line?
3. Can we ever give satisfying answers to questions about death?

# No More Getting Old

The older my friends and family get, the older I become. What an astute observation on my part! A few years ago, I reconnected by phone with a friend of forty years. When we first met, I was in my mid-twenties and she was in her mid-thirties. When my retired friend shared her age with me, I immediately said, "Stop. I don't want you to age anymore. I don't like this. I want you to stop growing older." She laughed loudly.

The ridiculousness of my statements was all too apparent. Failure to grow older meant that she would die. When I went on to say that I could not believe she was in her early seventies, she responded, "I can't believe you're in your sixties."

If we are fortunate to live, we grow older and discover that many of our family members are no longer with the living, except in our memories. Our memory pictures of people, places, and experiences remain static. We remember the way it was.

Those living into their eighties and nineties have outlived their contemporaries. They have more family and friends in the grave than friends above the grave. Often, I have heard their yearning for reunion with departed parents, spouses, and children. Asking why I am still living is common. What good am I? Don't mourn me when I'm gone; I'll be with my loved one.

The biblical story includes Enoch, the great-grandfather of Noah, who walked with God. I heard years ago the illustration that Enoch walked and talked with God each day. Each day Enoch ventured farther away from his earthly home. One day God said to Enoch, "We are closer to my home than yours. Come with me." Enoch went to be with God.

Aging, death, and grief are a part of our human existence. We cannot escape them.

## Questions to Ponder

1. What are your greatest fears about death?
2. Is it healthy to live with the awareness that death will eventually come?
3. What comforts do Christians have about death?
4. How can we walk with those whose death is imminent?
5. How do we minister to those in grief?

# Comforter of Those in Grief

Comforter of those in grief, we bow our heads with tears in our eyes and heaviness in our words for the loss we know. One no longer lives with us who was our friend, our brother, our sister, our parent, or our child. Some of these are well known and others are strangers to us, but we grieve for the loss of their lives and for the grief of their friends and families. One death has widening impacts for all. What might have been is no more. Familiar smiles, familiar frowns, familiar handshakes, familiar greetings, and familiar goodbyes live now in our individual and corporate memories. We do not know what to say. Give us the wisdom to simply be there for those in grief.

Scripture says that you will be with us until the ends of the world. It appears the world has ended as we know it. Thank you for being with us, not only in spirit but in others who follow you. Heal us with your providence; death no longer has the final victory. Ultimate victory lives in the reality and the power of the resurrection as shown in Jesus the Christ. Keep us close to each other as we grieve. Keep us close to you as we grieve with one another. Praise to the one who said we would not be left comfortless. For your comfort in the name of Jesus the Crucified, we pray. Amen.

# TIMES OF DEDICATION
# AND RENEWAL

*I beseech you therefore, brethren, by the mercies of God, that ye present your bodies a living sacrifice, holy, acceptable unto God, which is your reasonable service. And be not conformed to this world: but be ye transformed by the renewing of your mind, that ye may prove what is that good, and acceptable, and perfect, will of God.*
—Romans 12:1-2


*We never live so intensely as when we love strongly. We never realize ourselves so vividly as when we are in the full glow of love for others.*
—Walter Rauschenbusch


*He who conquers himself is the mightiest warrior.*
—Confucius

She was the pastor's wife and she played the piano beautifully. I would listen and wish that I had her talent. I had done that with numerous people, looking at their talent and wishing it were mine. One day it dawned on me that behind that talent were incredible hours of discipline. Practice. Practice. Practice.

Often, we look upon ability and fail to recognize that it, too, is a gift that was nurtured. Quite frankly, if I wanted to learn to play the piano, especially if I wanted to play beautifully, I would have to practice. I would have to learn the rudiments of music. Did I want to do that? Or did I just want to wish to play beautifully? I could not have one without the other; what I lacked was dedication. Wishes without actions are in vain.

My envy alone did not produce the attitude and actions required to play the piano. If we wish to refine those talents and abilities we possess, we must be willing to invest the time, energy, and basic discipline. We can easily say that doctors practice medicine and lawyers practice law. We practice many things. Sometimes we are successful; sometimes we are not. Jesus taught that if we would be the greatest, we must be a servant to all. Being a useful servant does not occur automatically or capriciously. Do we practice being a servant? What we fail to recognize is that life is a practice as well. We practice life as we practice anything else. We need elements of correction and feedback as we practice the Christian journey.

Within the first six weeks in Ogbomosho, Nigeria, I had become discouraged at my first full-time teaching assignment. I felt like a failure and wondered if I would be deported back to the United States. Employment as a grocery store bagger did not appeal to me! I had spent years in preparation, and after six weeks, I felt discouraged and questioned my vocation. What helped me tremendously was Paul's message to Timothy (2 Timothy 3:14): "continue thou in the things which thou has learned." I had to *keep on keeping on*, as the expression goes. As I kept keeping on, something miraculous happened. I began to criticize myself, my colleagues, and my students less. The classroom became a better experience. I learned from my mistakes, and I could acknowledge my successes. The joy of teaching returned.

So it is with faith. We need renewal that comes through times of quiet reflection and times of hard work, even when evidences of success are nonexistent. Practicing this type of life requires courage and fortitude. It requires movement from the known to the unknown and from the conscious to the unconscious. New faith comes as we practice the old through the rudimentary principles of love and service to all. Periodically we need worship services focusing on dedication and renewal. We may find that sustaining dedication leads to renewal.

The following pages provide supplemental resources that might enhance the preparation and celebration of dedication and renewal. You will find several hymns, readings, stories and theological reflections, and a seasonal prayer. May these resources become a seasoning to add new flavor to this important celebration. May you experience new imaginations, insights, and actions.

# Ability, Talent Surround Me, O Lord

**Claude Douglas Bryan**
Suggested Tune: ST. DENIO
Meter: 11.11.11.11.

Ability, talent surround me, O Lord;
Abundant gifts possible only from thee;
My offerings seem meager and low for my Lord;
Instruct me, O Lord, what to thee I can bring.

Two brothers once brought gifts of sacrifice free;
Each diff'rent in quality and in their call;
For one well received, and one caution bestowed;
By doing well, Cain, too, acceptance would find.

We know not why some gifts more sacred appear;
Our questions seek answers not easily found;
Our attitudes, like that of Cain, we must guard,
With thankfulness, modesty, giving to thee.

I ponder again now what has been bestowed,
Uniquely and wonderf'ly crafted for me;
Not simply my joy, but for all to enjoy
With all who have need of our God's holy touch.

Not one single gift can be worthy of thee
Than giving the one Gift entrusted to me;
Returning my blessings, to give him my all;
My legacy, sharing my gifts is God's call.

# Journeys of New Faith

**Claude Douglas Bryan**

**Suggested Tunes: MELITA**
**ST. PETERSBURG**
**ST. CATHERINE**
**Meter: 8.8.8.8.8.8.**

Christ summons journeys of new faith
For all who hear his holy call;
Away from safety wrenching us
To spheres unknown he calls us forth;
We know that thou will be our guide;
In thee our future shall reside.

We cannot follow thy commands
Unless we leave our wealth behind,
To gain new treasures bought by thee.
Relinquish we our former ways,
What we clasp dearly in our hands.
Trust we our lives to thy good care.

Our journey may not lead to lands
Away from family and friends;
Our calling may be to remain,
To be transformed where we live;
By thy grace living out from us,
We alter hearts of lives we touch.

Lord give us strength to do thy will;
Grant vision as thy guiding light;
Encourage us along our way,
Endow us with thy fellowship;
Move restless spirits within us
That we might find thy perfect peace."

# Living Wonders of His Love

**Claude Douglas Bryan**

**Suggested Tunes: BEECHER
BEACH SPRING
Meter: 8.7.8.7.D.**

Stand we now before the Father,
Faith in him has made us one.
Face these moments all together;
Holy vision shall be done.
Strength comes from thy perfect glory;
Wise are those who seek thy face.
Claim we power of thy presence;
May thy Word we all embrace.

Solve our deepest fears of race;
Bridge the languages we speak;
Join as one through newfound grace;
Give us courage to be meek.
Now remember Christ who died
That we might know harmony.
Change our faithless, misplaced pride;
Help us find tranquility.

May our days' and years' ambition
Show the fruits of life in thee.
May we live our one true mission—
Letting God's love flowing free.
Let us share this holy healing
With those longing to be whole.
God has claimed us for his purpose,
Living wonders of his love.

# To Share in Love and Sing Our Part

**Claude Douglas Bryan**          **Suggested Tunes: HE LEADETH ME**
**JERUSALEM**
**Meter: 8.8.8.8. with Chorus**

God's breath changed darkness into
  light;
Dark waters parted by his might.
The Father's song made life begin;
Parts given that the world might
  sing.
Our God and Lord still sings today;
The Word and Spirit guide the way.
Now open both our mind and
  heart
To share in love and sing our part.

Creations have their own true voice
That grows but God gives us the
  choice
To follow him and give our all
And join the chorus of God's call.
Our God and Lord still sings today;
The Word and Spirit guide the way.
Now open both our mind and
  heart
To share in love and sing our part.

To find our voice, both true and
  right,
We face the struggles, day and
  night;
Our voices cannot find true rest
Until we meet our daily test.
Our God and Lord still sings today;
The Word and Spirit guide the way.
Now open both our mind and
  heart
To share in love and sing our part.

Our song is not for us alone;
This gift from God is ours on loan;
The voice, this message, we must
  speak
To both the mighty and the meek.
Our God and Lord still sings today;
The Word and Spirit guide the way.
Now open both our mind and
  heart
To share in love and sing our part.

# Holy Spirit (Responsive Reading)

LEADER: "A new heart also will I give you, and a new spirit will I put within you: and I will take away the stony heart out of your flesh, and I will give you an heart of flesh" (Ezekiel 36:26).

PEOPLE: Give us a new heart and a new spirit.

LEADER: "But the Comforter, which is the Holy Ghost, whom the Father will send in my name, he shall teach you all things, and bring all things to your remembrance, whatsoever I have said unto you" (John 14:26).

PEOPLE: Teach us all things.

LEADER: "Then Peter said unto them, Repent, and be baptized every one of you in the name of Jesus Christ for the remission of sins, and ye shall receive the gift of the Holy Ghost" (Acts 2:38).

PEOPLE: We turn to you, Lord.

LEADER: "But ye shall receive power, after that the Holy Ghost is come upon you: and ye shall be witnesses unto me both in Jerusalem, and in all Judaea, and in Samaria, and unto the uttermost part of the earth" (Acts 1:8).

PEOPLE: Give us power and witness.

LEADER: "I have yet many things to say unto you, but ye cannot bear them now" (John 16:12).

PEOPLE: Tell us what we should know.

LEADER: "Now the Lord is that Spirit: and where the Spirit of the Lord is, there is liberty" (2 Corinthians 3:17).

PEOPLE: Thank you for this great liberty.

LEADER: "What? know ye not that your body is the temple of the Holy Ghost which is in you, which ye have of God, and ye are not your own?" (1 Corinthians 6:19)

 

**PEOPLE:** May the Spirit live within us.

LEADER: "If ye then, being evil, know how to give good gifts unto your children: how much more shall your heavenly Father give the Holy Spirit to them that ask him?" (Luke 11:13)

**PEOPLE:** Fill us with your Spirit.

LEADER: "If ye love me, keep my commandments" (John 14:15).

**PEOPLE:** Help us to keep your commandments.

LEADER: "But the fruit of the Spirit is love, joy, peace, longsuffering, gentleness, goodness, faith, meekness, temperance: against such there is no law" (Galatians 5:22-23).

**PEOPLE:** May we experience the fruit of the Spirit.

LEADER: "Likewise the Spirit also helpeth our infirmities: for we know not what we should pray for as we ought: but the Spirit itself maketh intercession for us with groanings which cannot be uttered" (Romans 8:26).

**PEOPLE:** Teach us what we should pray.

LEADER: "Now the God of hope fill you with all joy and peace in believing, that ye may abound in hope, through the power of the Holy Ghost" (Romans 15:13).

*ALL:* Amen.

# I Want Renewal (Monologue)

I want renewal. Yes, that's what I what. Renewal. I remember the Bible story about God asking Solomon what he wanted. Solomon asked for wisdom. God gave him wisdom. Solomon became famous for his wisdom throughout the centuries. I want renewal. I don't expect to become as well known for my renewal or remembered for hundreds of years, as Solomon was remembered. But that's what I want. That's what I need—renewal.

It's wonderful to finally know what I want. Renewal. But I don't want a loud renewal. I think I would prefer a softer version, not one quite so loud. I would like a good voice but not an overly loud voice. I don't want it to be too soft either. Yes, that's what I want—a moderate voice in my renewal. I understand that people often go to various places in the world when they experience renewal. But I don't like to travel, and I don't have a passport. In fact, I don't want to go through the inoculations that might be necessary. I would like renewal that does not involve travel, one that is just local. Yes, local is good. Local means that I'm dealing with my immediate neighborhood, with my Jerusalem. Yes, I would like renewal that is confined to my Jerusalem. But I want to be in the right neighborhood in Jerusalem. Some neighborhoods are too dangerous, and I just don't like the smell. Yes, a nice-smelling neighborhood is where I'd like to live with my renewal.

Now, I don't want to give up any of my current friends. I know that some people do when they experience renewal. But I would like the type of renewal that allows me to keep my old acquaintances because they, too, need to have my witness and my ministry. Besides, many new people sometimes make me feel uneasy. I'm basically shy, and I don't want to have to go to uncomfortable places when I'm renewed. Yes, I like renewal that focuses on the familiar. I can deal with familiar. Nothing new and nothing too fancy, just familiar. That's what I want.

I've been in school a long time, and I was sure glad when it was over. I would like a renewal that doesn't require a lot of reading. I mean, I'm okay reading the Bible, you know, and the Sunday school lesson. I think that's about all I really want to give attention to. I'll read the Bible and nothing else. I already know a lot about the Bible. It would be okay to learn a little bit more. I don't like change, and so I don't really want to focus on passages that might cause me to change. I don't want to rethink anything. No, I think the best witness is when we are comfortable with people and adapt to what they already know. Challenge is overrated and not required of everybody. Don't you think?

Well, I guess that's about all I can think of right now. Lord, send me renewal. I've talked about my preferences but again whatever you wish is fine with me. But I know that you're always considerate of what the other person wants, so I'll just expect what I said to be acceptable to you. If not, you can let me know. When do you think, Lord, I can expect this renewal to come? Will it be in the morning or the evening? I think I would prefer for renewal to come in the morning; that way I would start my day off right. If it came at night, I might be too excited and so I wouldn't sleep well. I think we should all have a good sleep before we get renewed. Thanks, God.

## In Like a Tortoise

The fourth week of the school year was over. The youth minister observed that some of the younger youth were becoming discouraged and overwhelmed. They were just entering high school from middle school. They were changing classes, keeping up with assignments, making new friends, learning how to get around the building, and making decisions about their future educational plans through course selections. What path would they choose?

Now that they were part of the youth group, they were challenged by their church leaders to read their Bible daily; to have fellowship with each other; to study their Sunday school material; to spend time in prayer for themselves, family, friends, church, and others; to discover God's will concerning vocation; to keep physically active; to eat well-balanced meals; to make new friends; and to become involved with churchwide activities as well as specific youth activities. *Wow!* thought the youth minister. *No wonder they feel overwhelmed.*

"I just can't keep up!" one highly frustrated girl proclaimed. Several others joined in her pronouncement.

The youth minister began telling them the traditional story of the tortoise and the hare in the hopes of conveying the message of taking things one step at a time. He could tell that he wasn't making contact with them. Down-turned heads were his first clue. "Scratch that one," he said. "Let me tell you a real story that happened to me."

He explained that he had been an average to slightly above-average student in elementary school and middle school. No pressures at all. He was accepted. Then, suddenly, he was in his first year of high school and was being bullied in the classroom by his peers. At the end of his freshman year, his grades were slightly above average—C's and a few B's. He envied the students who spoke of lofty vocational aspirations. He wanted to "make something out of himself." He knew he needed to get into classes where there were fewer behavioral problems and more educational opportunities. He wanted to achieve.

He knew he could not automatically go from a grade point average of 2.2 to one closer to 4.0. He set incremental goals for himself. First, he said to himself that during his sophomore year he would make nothing less than a B. He accomplished this goal. Gradually he was placed in more advanced classes. In his junior year he decided that this year he would only have A's and B's. In his senior year he said to himself that he would have more A's than B's. He discovered that if the goals were realistic and he worked hard, then they were attainable for him. He did not make the National Honor Society his junior year as many of his new friends did. However, at the end of his senior year he was inducted into the society.

"Now, is that better than the tortoise and the hare?" the youth minister asked. "I was able to handle everything with one step at a time. You can, too."

## Questions to Ponder

1. Can spiritual goals be accomplished incrementally? If so, how?
2. Can we take on too much at one time? Explain.

# Beneath the Radar

Radar, first used in World War I, detected incoming bomber flights. Flying above the radar meant detection and possible destruction; flying below the radar meant going unnoticed and having possible success. The expression became popular in everyday language and everyday situations. Keeping your head below radar meant that you would not be detected.

Throughout the centuries, Christians communities have experienced division along theological and social issues. Culture wars abound; shifts in thinking occur. I knew friends, colleagues, and former teachers who approached their employment at educational institutions with temerity. Should their personal theological positions be different from that of the administration and trustees, they would use care in what they said in the classroom and especially what they said in print.

Some were beginning their careers, others were mid-career, and others were nearing retirement. Their thoughts included if I can just gain a few years of experience, I can then look elsewhere; if I could just achieve tenure with its guarantee of employment or at least obstacles in dismissal; if I can just get my youngest child through college through a tuition exchange program; and if I can stay on until Medicare is available. They would "hunker down" and live a life and career undetected as long possible. I suppose we all play this hunker-down strategy at times.

When I asked a former colleague how his department could maintain its mission at a certain religiously conservative institution, he said, "We try to keep below radar."

I smiled and pondered his words. *Must be hard to stand tall*, I thought.

While the Christian faith would teach the importance of humility and not calling attention to ourselves, it would also speak of not hiding our light under a basket. Christian lives may be lived below the radar of detection, either intentionally or unintentionally. If done unintentionally, it may be that words and acts would not indicate to others that we are living up to God-given and God-directed intention. Torn between the two, we must decide. Are we being called to slouch? Are we being called to rise? Emily Dickinson's poem "We never know how high we are" challenges and encourages. How can we stand tall? We do not know what we will achieve unless we respond to the challenges before us. Fears may hinder; courage allows us to respond. How do we measure up to God's grand design?

## Questions to Ponder

1. What qualities does it take to live above the radar?
2. What occurs when we live below the radar?
3. To whose advantage and disadvantage is our living below the radar?

# God of Night and Day

God of night and day, light and darkness, we thank you for creation's designs that show both the beginning and the ending of each day. Just as a musician or athlete must practice their art daily, we, too, must practice the art of living. Help us to be faithful to the gifts and opportunities before us. May the words and thoughts that dance in our minds reveal encouragement and compassion, not despair and desolation. As Scripture indicates, your messengers speak with words of not being afraid. Help us not to be afraid to be who we might be as part of a creation far greater than our comprehension.

May we learn to find moments of renewal and to reclaim the grace that is made available to each of us, to our church, and to our institutions. Keep within us the spirit of possibility that allows us to grow freely, boldly, and faithfully. Transform obstacles into opportunities. Deliver us from the grief of what might have been to the joy of what is. Give us the fortitude to stand tall within and for your Kingdom. May we lift others up. Keep us renewed. In the name of Jesus the Crucified, we pray. Amen.

# TIMES OF DEPARTURE

*Go ye therefore, and teach all nations, baptizing them in the name of the Father, and of the Son, and of the Holy Ghost…*
—Matthew 28:19

*Only in the agony of parting do we look into the depths of love.*
—George Eliot

*Take only what you need and leave the land as you found it.*
—Arapaho saying

Entrances and exits are a part of our daily lives. When we enter and when we leave, new stories or dramas are initiated. In *As you Like It*, Act 2, Scene 7, William Shakespeare penned the lines, "All the world's a stage, and all the men and women merely players: they have their exits and their entrances; and one man in his time plays many parts, his acts being seven ages" (at *The Complete Works of Shakespeare*, http://shakespeare.mit.edu/). Major or minor, our lives are filled with comings and goings. Entrances and exits occur with church congregations and other communities of faith.

Psychological research verifies that first impressions are important. First impressions can establish the tone for relationships, for orientations, and for listening. Quick assessments leading to bad first impressions may be difficult to overcome or correct. While not impossible to correct, first impressions do influence future relationships. Just as care must be exercised in how one is welcomed into a place such as a congregation, care should be given to departures.

While we may have an opportunity to correct first impressions, we do not have the luxury of retakes for a departure. Departures occur for a variety of reasons—some beyond the individual's control or intention. In both the Old and New Testaments we have examples of people moving on in their journeys. Biblical examples are often described in grandiose styles such as Elijah who walked with God or the Hebrew children's departure from Egyptian slavery. Other departures may be unnoticed as one escapes into the night, such as Joseph's taking his family to Egypt.

Some departures are developmental or anticipated, such as graduation or relocation to another place where physical, mental, and social needs might be met in another community. Departures can also be a commissioning to a new place of witness and ministry. Departures may not be wanted or self-initiated, such as the deportation of the people of Israel and Judah. Not everyone has the privilege to initiate their departure from life's various stages.

As important as the impressions on entrance, departures allow for appreciation of present relationships, closure to a segment of life, and the opportunity to begin a new phase. Departures are a part of the life of the church. If the church has opportunity, it should find ways to make departures meaningful for those who are leaving and those left behind. How we are treated on departing influences future returns.

The following pages provide supplemental resources that might enhance the preparation for observing those who physically depart. You will find several hymns, readings, stories and reflections, and a seasonal prayer. May these resources become a seasoning to add new flavor to this important event. May you experience new imaginations, insights, and actions.

# For Friendships Sweet

**Claude Douglas Bryan**

**Suggested Tunes: DIX
LUX PRIMA
RATISBON
REDHEAD
Meter: 7.7.7.7.7.7.**

In the travels of our day,
God brings friends to bless our
  way;
Ones who share with us their love,
Surely come from him above.
Grateful for the ones we meet,
Thank you, God, for friendships
  sweet.

Faithful friends who watch and
  care,
Help in what we each must bear.
Friends at worship, work, and play
Bring us joy in each new day.
Grateful for the ones we meet,
Thank you, God, for friendships
  sweet.

Friends who teach and share their
  art
Live by love from God's own heart.
Faith in Christ will set us free.
Friends help find what we should
  be.
Grateful for the ones we meet,
Thank you, God, for friendships
  sweet.

Friends near change us day by day
Into God's more perfect way.
Holy Spirit moves in each
To bring peace within our reach.
Grateful for the ones we meet,
Thank you, God, for friendships
  sweet.

God may call us to depart;
We take each one in our heart.
Treasures are the days we share,
Praise to Him, the first to care.
Grateful for the ones we meet,
Thank you, God, for friendships
  sweet.

## Distant Yet Connected

**Claude Douglas Bryan**                    **Suggested Tune: DIX**
**Meter:** 7.7.7.7.7.7.

For the hardships felt today, separations we must face,
Calling forth our deepest faith, knowing, living through God's grace.
Jesus shows God's boundless care, finds us living ev'rywhere.

For the folding of each day, for the challenge faced this year,
Daily nature shows its force, illness thrives across the sphere.
Jesus shows God's boundless care, finds us living ev'rywhere.

Hearing news beyond belief, neither we nor church the same.
Actions show and words reveal, causing pride or causing shame.
Jesus shows God's boundless care, finds us living ev'rywhere.

Minds and spirits must unite, faith and reason, our friends true,
Both can offer guidance new, showing love, we each must do.
Jesus shows God's boundless care, finds us living ev'rywhere.

Through these darkened paths may we carry lights of hope to all,
Distant yet connected still, we renew our godly call.
Jesus shows God's boundless care, finds us living ev'rywhere.

# Part of Your Journey (Responsive Reading)

LEADER: Jesus instructed that as we are traveling to go into the world, we should go proclaiming the Gospel. Opportunities exist, but those willing to respond are few. We join to recognize _____________'s answer to the opportunities of God. We are pleased to be a part of journey.

**PEOPLE:** We are a part of your journey.

LEADER: We pray that God will be in your going, in your staying, and in your returning. We are a part of your journey.

**PEOPLE:** We are a part of your journey.

LEADER: We charge you in the journey to go in the power of God, in the love and support of this congregation. Will you so go?

*CANDIDATE:* I will.

LEADER: We pledge our prayers, our thoughts, and our support to you in this journey.

**PEOPLE:** We are a part of your journey.

LEADER: We commission you to go into the world with the light of Christ and to be the Christ to all you encounter. Always remember, you are not alone.

**PEOPLE:** We are a part of your journey.

LEADER: Go in the fullness of God's peace and the support of God's people.

*ALL:* We are a part of your journey.

   

# A Departing Commission (Charge)

God of the Matriarchs and Patriarchs, Sarah and Abraham, Rebekah and Isaac, Rachel, Leah, and Jacob, we ask your blessing and presence for these loved ones going from our congregation. Those of faith are often called upon to travel to places and to people unknown. New opportunities and necessities pull or push us forward from the known to the unknown.

We are grateful for the time and the energy they have invested in serving you through this congregation. Thank you for the gifts you have given them and for their willingness to share those gifts with us and the greater community of faith. We know that their presence cannot be replaced. We will remember their unique contributions to our fellowship. Everyone helps us to understand God's love and the various expressions of the gift of life and service. May we have been an accepting fellowship that has promoted both growth and challenge, acceptance and gratitude.

Guide them as they depart from us. Help them to remember the friendship and the fellowship they have experienced here. Grant them the courage to make new friendships and to experience new fellowship in the days ahead. Allow them to be patient with themselves in their adjustments to new circumstances and new people. Provide the resources, both tangible and intangible, to aid them in their journey.

As we say goodbye, we wish them the absolute best for the future. Help them to recall the words of Jesus: "Lo, I am with you always." In the name of Jesus the Christ we pray. Amen.

# Eleven Roses

He was leaving college for a few days prior to his formal graduation. These friends would not be at school when he returned for graduation. Compared to his high school experience, he had flourished in college—not in academic achievement but in being a part of a loving, supportive, and fun community. Knowing he would be saying goodbye to the familiar friends of four years was painful. How could he say goodbye, especially to the females of the clique? He calculated how many females would be invited to the time of his sendoff. Eleven. He ordered eleven roses. As he prepared to get in the car to leave, he gave to each of his female friends a rose.

## Questions to Ponder

1. What is your most memorable goodbye? What made it positive? What made it negative?
2. How should a church respond to a church member who is leaving?
3. Are goodbyes and hellos related?

 

## Taking Leave

One of my favorite country-western song comes from the film *The Gambler*. You may recall the key ideas in playing cards—hold, fold, walk, and run. A more sacred account may be found in the book of Ecclesiastes with its list of "a time to…." These depictions stress the importance of decision-making. Jesus acknowledges that there are times to "shake off the dust" (Matthew 10:14 and Mark 6:11) when needed. When do we move on?

Abraham's faith journey, recorded in the twelfth chapter of the book of Genesis, reveals the twists and turns in leading a family to the promised land. No simple answer or formula exists. Included within these dynamics is the plight of his nephew, Lot. Lot chose to leave his uncle's family, he chose to take bounty of the family possessions, and he chose to live in a city noted for inhospitality to the stranger. Were these poor choices? We later learn that Lot and family were rescued from unhealthy situations.

Much of life is filled with the agony of choice. I do not make major choices easily. I spend much time thinking before leaping. My first secretary laughed when she noticed that I meticulously calculated each student's grade three times before recording the final semester average. I tried to grade my student papers in one setting for uniformity of grading conditions. I would think and rethink, sometimes agonizing over the grade recorded. Grading rubrics helped, but there was still agony before recording the grade in ink. In my defense, I can say that once recorded, I did not look back and doubt the grades given. If a student requested, I would reexamine and recalculate the grades. But once the decision was made, I did not second-guess myself. My agony was wisely invested in making the decision and not in second-guessing the decision.

Knowing when to depart from a relationship, a place of employment, a friendship, or a church is even more challenging than knowing what grade to give. When I am in doubt, I have made no choice. I am prone to stay in the course of decisions, even when toxicity is becoming apparent.

How can we know when to leave? The simple answer is to ask God. Honest answers to questions may be helpful. Does my staying in this current situation promote health and wellness for all? Can I make a realistic difference at this time? Is my overall Christian witness increased by my staying or my going? Are my values congruent with the messages and behaviors of the group? What role is fear playing in my decision-making? Have I given my reasonable and best investment? What have been the returns? What is my vision for the future? With limited time, where should I invest my energies? These are the types of questions I ponder as I ask God. Complex behind-the-scenes work can make the answer simple.

## Questions to Ponder

1. How do you know when it is time to leave a place?
2. How do you know when it is time to leave a relationship?
3. What do you say to those struggling to make a weighty decision that may involve departure?

## God of Abraham and Sarah

God of Abraham and Sarah, Isaac and Rebekah, Paul and Mary Magdalene, Aquila and Priscilla, and God in Jesus the Christ, we come acknowledging your lordship of our journey. You are the God who calls each of us to journey. Not only do we journey with you geographically, but we also journey with you in how we live and in how we treat one another. Journeys are not always easy or welcomed. Some journeys are planned; others are extemporaneous. We move to places uniquely prepared for us.

Thank you for the friendships made, for shared moments of joy and sadness, and for activities held in common. Protect those who are called to move away and those called to stay. Thank you for the days ahead with new friendships and new journeys. May we take away the best memories, experiences, and lessons learned. May we wish well to the past and to the future. Keep us focused on what lies ahead. May we desire the best for those who stay behind and those who move ahead. Be with us in the twists and turns of the journey, knowing that others left behind are on a journey as well. May the day come when we are together once more. For the goings and the comings, in the name of Jesus the Crucified we pray. Amen.

# TIMES OF DISCERNMENT

*Beloved, believe not every spirit, but try the spirits whether they are of God: because many false prophets are gone out into the world.*
—1 John 4:1

*Wisdom is oftentimes nearer when we stoop than when we soar.*
—William Wordsworth

*Pay attention to the whispers, so we won't have to listen to the screams.*
—Cherokee proverb

Churches, like individuals, often face crises that demand a choice. Discerning the right choice is important. Some choices come expectedly and routinely; others are unplanned and unusual. One of my favorite background stories of hymn construction is associated with the hymn "Once to Every Man and Nation" by James Russell Lowell. This hymn was penned around the annexation question faced by the United States with the Mexican territories in 1845. The moment to decide is important.

Permanent decisions are not easily made. In some religious traditions, one thinking of entering full-time ministry goes through a period of discernment. In discernment, honesty, self-evaluation, peer evaluations, and experiences in ministry occur. This choosing involves intense times of spiritual challenges.

Our choices may sometimes gain the favor of the masses; other times our choices will result in the disfavor of the masses. An important question is what would please or displease God. This question is not easily answered with honesty. We struggle to know. Hopefully, these decisions are made through honest dialogue with God and with others. Church welfare considers the impact of choices on the individuals and the overall group. Choices produce character in individuals and in the larger community. Churches gain reputations, either good or bad, for their decisions, especially in the treatment of ministerial staff.

Helping individuals to make sound, private decisions is an important skill that each church member should be equipped to do. Congregation-governed churches must make decisions in the context of a group. Leading a congregation in the discernment process is time-consuming. Specialized training and practice are needed in learning to hear the spoken messages and unspoken messages of each member. While each member may not have "his or her own way," each member should be heard respectfully. Achieving consensus and commitment is foundational. Congregational life is one of the great experiments conducted within God's Kingdom. Can we choose wisely, knowing that our choices affect not only our generation but also the younger generations who watch us? Knowing how to discern is critical to any organization, including the corporate life of the individual congregation, especially those who are independent and autonomous. Wise, trusted, and mature leadership is needed.

The following pages provide supplemental resources that might enhance the preparation for important discernment or decision-making. You will find several hymns, readings, stories and theological reflections, and a seasonal prayer. May these resources become a seasoning to add new flavor to this important event. May you find new imaginations, insights, and actions.

# Lord, Guard and Guide Us in This Fateful Day

**Claude Douglas Bryan**

**Suggested Tunes: EVENTIDE**
**MORECAMBRE**
**Meter: 10.10.10.10.**

Lord, guard and guide us in this fateful day;
Stay near with light to show thy holy way.
A touch from thee, hear now our one appeal—
Once more again thy Son in us reveal.

Sorrows and sins today we need confess;
Lives broken in our midst we must address
To One who shows his living grace can heal
Heartbreaks of ev'ryone and human ill.

The world now waits and watches for our acts;
May paths of truth and mercy be not lax.
Stand strong may we and speak in courage free;
Faith's tests of love and Christ abide in thee.

Keep us near thee; if not we stray and fall.
Temptations near pose threats to one and all.
By day and night we pray to pass the test;
Show us your answers, grant us peaceful rest.

# We Look Upon Our World and Wonder

**Claude Douglas Bryan**                    **Suggested Tune: ELLERS**
**Meter: 10.10.10.10.**

We look upon our world and wonder why—
Why hesitate we to show right from wrong?
Why craft we monuments at man's expense?
Why discontent and turmoil are with us?

We look upon our world and wonder what—
What difference our own response will make?
What part can we play when evil abounds?
What message can we bring to this our place?

We look upon our world and wonder who—
Who can heal hurt and pain of fractured lives?
Who can be valiant for the innocent?
Who can do what we alone cannot do?

We look upon our world and wonder when—
When gender will define not work we do?
When race and wealth will measure not our worth?
When bonds of love in Christ will hold us firm?

We look upon our world and wonder where—
Where can we find true worship for our souls?
Where do reason and compassion coexist?
Where can we live in faith and brotherhood?

The world we live in is like one found by Christ;
Society lacks harmony with thee.
We may not find all answers that we seek;
We live between earth and heaven above.

We shall find solace in this one great truth—
For God in Christ became our advocate.
The advocates, too, for all we must be,
By this we may find answers that we seek.

# In Youth (Poem)

In youth we ask questions,
Expecting adulthood to provide answers.
Adulthood shows that more questions remain.
Closer to death, our questions still persist.
No longer anxious or plagued, we wait in peace.

## Questions to Ponder

1. Do adults and youth discern God's directions differently? Explain.
2. Do you make use of different processes or questions of discernment now as compared to when you were younger? If so, explain those differences.
3. How does a person of faith determine God's will? Explain.

# The Dance (Poem)

Mixed feelings dance as partners within my soul,
One takes a step, another one follows.
Leads often change depending upon music played,
Making movement across the floor.

Joy and fear, unlikely but constant partners,
Vying for the power to take the lead,
One step forward, two steps backward,
Learning to dance with incompatibilities.

Hearing the call from the one Caller,
Knowing how to follow as rhythm leads,
Sometimes clearly, sometimes awkwardly,
Perfection not, but moving with imperfections.

Prices for the dances we choose,
Dime a dance or much, much more.
Costs paid not by money alone;
Our soul may be charged the price.

## Questions to Ponder

1. What could the dance represent?
2. Have you ever been out of step with those dancing in the room around you? Explain.
3. How can we dance with God?
4. What is the price of dancing?

 

# The Escalator

The young boy lived in a small town where no stores had escalators. While there might be a service elevator, his experience was wide wooden stairways between the floors. His mother took him for an adventure to the larger city where his grandparents lived. One day they took the boy to a large department store with merchandise on each floor for the home and for the individual. These floors were connected by an escalator.

He was fascinated by everything he saw. He asked his mother if he could explore. She said yes, but stay close. He walked around the third floor of the store and saw the escalator. He went down the escalator and explored the second floor. Then he knew he had to go back to his mother. He returned to the escalator that had brought him down to the second floor.

Looking up, he took initial steps up the escalator, but it was going down. Each step forward brought him further back down to the second floor. He wanted to go to the next floor. People were coming down and he alone was trying to go up. Overwhelmed and frustrated, he began to cry when he could not make progress upward. Suddenly he saw a woman who outstretched her hand to him. He made progress toward her. He was able to clasp her hand and she said, "I'll help you." Together he and the stranger rode the escalator downward. She guided him to the right escalator going in the right direction.

At the top of the upward escalator, he saw his mother standing. He cried out, "Mother." The stranger guided him to put his first foot on the upward escalator and watched him move to the top. When he reached his mother, he turned around and waved to the stranger at the foot of the escalator.

## Questions to Ponder

1. What role did the stranger play in the young boy's dilemma?
2. What can we learn from the stranger?
3. How have others helped you find the right direction?
4. How are you helping others find the right direction?
5. Is there just one right direction?

# Internal Compass

"Stay north," I was told.

"Okay," I said. Without an in-car compass, I would have no possibility of staying north.

I admit that I have no innate sense of direction. I must go through a well-developed protocol to determine the simple directions of north, south, east, and west. My brain is not wired for direction. Fortunately, I am willing to ask for directions. "Hello, I'm directionally impaired." It is something that I have learned to laugh about rather than to unsuccessfully attempt to conceal. I am grateful for what I call external compasses.

In life we need an internal decision-making compass, not for physical directions alone but for making moral, social, financial, or relational choices. Our moral compass, developmental in nature, must be periodically calibrated based on the latest information, understanding, experiences, simple trial and error, and the leading of the Holy Spirit. Our different moral compasses help us to face the challenges of living with others in cooperation, respect, and community.

Learning to trust and to rely on our internal compass is important. Once in my career I faced the unpleasant reality of working under an immediate supervisor whose moral compass I truly believed was incompatible with mine. When the opportunity occurred to change supervisors, I did.

A well-calibrated moral compass should reflect and lead to the fullest measure of God's love, grace, and compassion. We need a moral living compass that we can trust, especially in times of darkness and uncertainty. Former military pilots have told me that a major mistake young pilots make is not to trust the plane's instruments. Well-developed moral compasses empowered by God's Spirit can provide trustful directions and comfort in times of doubt and questions.

## Questions to Ponder

1. What are the elements in your internal compass?
2. Who has contributed in developing your moral compass?
3. What experiences have altered your decision-making process?
4. Should Christians have common elements in their internal compasses?
5. Are differences in moral compasses beneficial? Explain.

   

# Guide and Guardian of our Days

Guide and Guardian of our days, be near and with us in these days of decision and discernment. Help us to clearly know the directions that we should follow [you may wish to include the specific decision before the church]. Assist us as we look for those windows, both open and closed, of opportunity, and the door, both open and closed, of commitment. May we become an honest people who can read the messages from you that surround us. Keep us on tracks of faithfulness and not simple convenience. Help us to know the rights and wrongs of the daily situations we encounter. Comfort us in our realizations that answers are not always simple and easy. The sinfulness and brokenness within us and within the world influence our efficacy of choices.

Help us not to be afraid to listen to information and ideas that would challenge both our thinking and our living. Help us not to be afraid to perform boldly in acts that may not always be with the sentiments of the crowd. Before we can lead others, we must learn to be led by you. May we take advantage of the counsel of the wise in our decision-making and not simply the world of the popular and the flamboyant. Help us to know when not to look back as we move forward. Comfort us in the knowledge that poor decisions are not beyond redemption and that good decisions must be faithfully followed. Direct and lead us in the name of Jesus the Crucified, we pray. Amen.

# TIMES OF EASTER AND RESURRECTION

*Jesus said unto her, I am the resurrection, and the life: he that believeth in me, though he were dead, yet shall he live: And whosoever liveth and believeth in me shall never die. Believest thou this?*
—John 11:25-26

*Spring bursts to-day, For Christ is risen and the earth's at play.*
—Christina G. Rosetti

*And he departed from our sight that we might return to our hearts, and find Him. For He left, and behold, He is here.*
—St. Augustine

Next to Christmas, the most prominently known Christian observance is Easter. Both days celebrate the birth and rebirth of Christ. Each day plays a vital role in our corporate Christian story and in our individual lives. Like Christmas, Easter has become commercialized, far from its original celebration.

The week's events are somewhat familiar to us, including the triumphal entry on Sunday; the cleansing of the temple on Monday; the debating with religious leaders on Tuesday; the conspiring of Judas Iscariot with authorities for Jesus' betrayal on Wednesday; the gathering for the Last Supper and the arrest on Thursday; the crucifying of Jesus on Friday; the mourning and despair on Saturday; and the moving from death into life though the resurrection celebration on Sunday. What a roller coaster of a week it was!

How do we live after Easter Sunday? What about this week and the coming weeks of our lives? Darkness and despair have been transformed into light and hope because of Easter Sunday. Easter transforms lives and living.

Those who celebrate, trust, and serve Jesus the Christ bring light to the world and to people who live in darkness. While each of our stories will be different, they will have common themes and common roles. We each have the risen Savior living mysteriously within us and guiding us. Even though God accepted us, we may not find acceptance in all spheres of life. Just as Jesus experienced rejection, we, too, may experience rejection.

We will be misunderstood and judged harshly by those outside of our religious community and, at times, more painfully by those within our religious community. In fact, our very lives will be a threat to those who have not been fully restored to life. We are called to live both in the light of day and in the dark of night. During these days between darkness and light and between night and day, may we celebrate Easter and the future Kingdom of God. Because of Easter, may we respond with the simplicity of another follower who was questioned and who simply responded, "I was blind, now I see" (John 9:25).

The following pages provide supplemental resources that might enhance the preparation for the celebration of Easter. You will find several hymns, readings, stories and theological reflections, and a seasonal prayer. May these resources become a seasoning to add new flavor to this important celebration. May you experience new imaginations, insights, and actions.

 

# Once More We Pause This Easter Morn

**Claude Douglas Bryan**

**Suggested Tunes: O WALY WALY**
**MARYTON**
**Meter: 8.8.8.8.**

Once more we pause this Easter morn,
As we recall the time long past;
Creation fell; all life stood still
And waited for the Master's touch.

A broken world in fragments torn,
Upheld by man's frail will and strength;
Her people searched for inward peace
And found not man's own sweet release.

In love our God looked down on us,
Became for us what we could not.
Forsook he heaven for our gain,
Revealed true love in sacrifice.

Forgetting not the heavy cost,
So each reborn may fully live;
Reveal to us, O Precious Lord,
The full extent of Calvary's love.

To know the cost that we must count,
To walk our Savior's perfect way;
To give up earthly pleasures dear,
To gain our richest Lord's acclaim.

Renew us now this day we pray,
That once reborn for service true,
And by thy love we are made one;
We live by faith thy wondrous call.

# Good News Has Found Us

**Claude Douglas Bryan**               **Suggested Tune: BUNNESSAN**
                                       **Meter: 5.5.5.3.D.**

Good News has found us,
Like the first hearers—
Held in the bondage,
Snared by our sin.
Praise for redemption!
Praise for the Kingdom!
Praise for the blessing!
Changed by the Blood!

God's grace has warmed us,
Clothed by his Spirit,
Clasped by the faithful,
Held by his Word.
Free in salvation,
Life for a lifetime,
Sharing his Mission—
Now we proclaim.

Easter has broken
Into our being.
Healing, restoring,
Setting us free.
Glory and honor,
Love and devotion,
Joyfully pledge we
New lives to thee.

# Lump of Clay II (Poem)

God kept faithful watch over all he made,
How the world and her people had decayed.
God sent the prophets to proclaim his way;
Still the hearts and minds of people would not sway.

God took a lump of clay
From earth one special day,
Giving new life and play
Into a lump of clay.

Till God's Son was born, lived, and died on earth;
Through Jesus' sacrifice we have rebirth.
Now we each have a chance to live again.
For God's grace and Good News, we say Amen.

Don't remain just a lump of clay,
Lost and alone on each new day.
Let Jesus find life in your heart,
Shaping you into heaven's art.

## Questions to Ponder

1. How does the author describe the role that God plays in life?
2. How would you respond to individuals who do not sense God's presence?
3. Is there danger in becoming more than a lump of clay? Explain.
4. What roles should we play in helping mold other lumps of clay?

   

## Easter Morning (Responsive Reading)

LEADER: Lord, we greet you this Sunday morning.

PEOPLE: What is special about today?

LEADER: This is the Sunday of all Sundays!

PEOPLE: Resurrection Day.

LEADER: We celebrate God's love for all people.

PEOPLE: God's love for all people.

LEADER: God loved us to show the Way into the Kingdom of God.

PEOPLE: God showed us the Way.

LEADER: We are now forever brothers and sisters in Jesus the Christ.

PEOPLE: Brothers and sisters.

LEADER: United we can meet God's challenges.

PEOPLE: What are these challenges?

LEADER: To go into all the world as we are able.

PEOPLE: To go into all the world as we are able.

LEADER: We are to tell all that we have learned of the Savior, Jesus the Christ.

PEOPLE: To tell all that we have learned of the Savior, Jesus the Christ.

LEADER: We are to learn to live as family and citizens within God's Kingdom.

PEOPLE: To live as family and citizens within God's Kingdom.

LEADER: Let us go and greet God and his loved ones.

PEOPLE: To go, to tell, and to live.

*ALL:* Amen.

# Easter People

Originally there were two groups of people who lived on the island. One group was known as the West-er people and the other as the East-er people. As you would imagine, the West-er people lived on the west side of the island and the East-er people lived on the east side of the island. The West-er people were the strongest, most well connected, prosperous, and powerful on the island. They were prone to aggression, subduing, killing, or banishing their enemies.

The more the East-er people suffered, the more they continued to grow. Sociologists noted that the birthrate of the West-er people was dramatically less than that of the East-er people. Population demographics changed, and now the two groups were more spread across their island home. Old memories and traditions continued despite modern advancements.

One day a child asked her mother, "Why do they call us the East-er people?"

"We're the East-er people," she said. "We keep showing up, even when it seems hopeless. We're like some weeds; you can't get rid of us. You can kill us, but we still live."

## Questions to Ponder

1. What does it mean to be an Easter people?
2. How did you become an Easter person?
3. Can all people become Easter people?

# Periodic Charts and Beyond

My first recollections of the large periodic chart at the front of the chemistry classroom are fascinating. Those charts identified known elements of the universe with various characteristics. I would later view printed charts depicting the life, the work, the death, the resurrection, and the return of Jesus. The book of Revelation has been put into outline form, describing major events occurring at the end of creation. No doubt all disciplines have such graphs and charts that seek to identify major elements and summations of the disciplines. Whatever the discipline, we are prone to identify, to depict, to understand, and to predict if possible.

The world is open to exploration. Theories are created as broad explanations for such items as events or behaviors. As a part of the scientific process, theories are our attempts to explain, predict, and control. From theories, the scientific perspective seeks to establish laws to govern phenomena. Not all phenomena are easily governed.

Resurrection defies human explanation. Life begets life; death begets nothing. Into this way of human understanding, God intervened through the death of Jesus Christ. Jesus Christ resurrected from death into life. The biblical messages declare that through grace, trust, and faith, we, too, can experience resurrection.

Thoughtful theologians across the centuries have developed various theories of atonement to explain the resurrection story. Why was it necessary for Jesus to die? Could human sin and brokenness be atoned in another way? What is the role of blood? What is the role of love? What type of God would require such sacrifice? How we think about these issues influences how we understand and describe God, how we treat other humans, how we witness, and how we contribute to the Kingdom of God.

Some phenomena cannot be reduced to rational human laws. We sometimes spend our time trying to take the mystery out of the unknown. While we may seek to explain, we must be careful not to explain away or to fail to acknowledge the mystery. How resurrection was accomplished is a mystery. We cannot understand it, predict it, or control it. We can only speculate. Resurrection occurs unexpectedly. It is to be enjoyed and shared and not to be explained.

## Questions to Ponder

1. Should we seek to understand and explain all phenomena?
2. If we can't explain something, should we dismiss it?
3. What mysteries of faith are beyond our understanding?
4. What do we do when we can't understand?

## God of the Sundays, Mondays, Tuesdays...

God of the Sundays, Mondays, Tuesdays, Wednesdays, Thursdays, Fridays, and Saturdays, we are gathered here on the Sunday of Sundays, Easter, to celebrate the love that Jesus the Christ showed us though his life, death, and resurrection. From a humble birth to a life of service, a sacrificial death, and a glorious resurrection, Jesus was God made flesh. This Jesus lived in the past, lives in the present, and will live in our future. Jesus reveals the embodiment of heavenly love made flesh. Joyfully we acknowledge this powerful love that sustains us from birth to life, to death, and to eternity. By faith and grace, we are linked forever.

In this time of corporate worship, may the spirit of resurrection live within each of us. Empower our words and our songs. Let praise abound. Help us to see with eyes and hearts renewed by the beauty of God's loving creation. May the sacrifices made not be in vain. May our lives experience resurrection, revealing Jesus in acts of forgiveness and comfort shown today and tomorrow. Transform our prejudices into acceptance; our apathy into love; and our mistakes into contrition. Your grace is open to all. May we live this day in celebration of a life resurrected, a life that dwells with you and through you. He is alive! He is alive! May we join those who herald the melodies of God's redeeming grace for now and forever. In the name of Jesus the Crucified, we pray. Amen.

# TIMES OF FAMILY DEDICATION AND RENEWAL

*When I call to remembrance the unfeigned faith that is in thee, which dwelt first in thy grandmother Lois, and thy mother Eunice; and I am persuaded that in thee also.*
—2 Timothy 1:5

*God's dream is that you and I and all of us will realize that we are family, that we are made for togetherness, for goodness, and for compassion.*
—Tecumseh

*The old woman looks after the child to grow its teeth and the young one in turn after the woman when she loses her teeth.*
—African Proverb

At one time it may have been much easier to define what constitutes a family. Today the designation defies a simple definition. But families may have always resisted the imposition of the definitions of others. The best definition may emerge from self-report and self-definition. If people declare themselves as family, they function as a family.

Families provide the initial framework for developing the individual's worldview. Families teach us how we are to regard ourselves, the world around us, our beliefs, and our actions. Families teach us to trust or mistrust, to love or hate, and to be brave or be fearful. Families have the power to give enrichment or to deprive members of their growth and individuality. Families can be opened or closed to others and the outside world.

The church consists of brothers and sisters, a new family. Achieving family is not a simple task, not a onetime event. Sustaining families involves tasks to provide enough cohesion to keep the individuals related and enough freedom to promote individual growth. Too much cohesion may result in enmeshment that prevents individuality. Church members, too, are shaped through the modeled behaviors of others. Through their interactions with fellow members, churches develop and reinforce certain worldviews. Those members embracing the church's worldview are accepted and reinforced. Those members who do not fully embrace the church's worldview may be rejected or ignored. Congregations, like families, may become known for certain characteristics or themes. A sense of church as family requires extended time to develop; its destruction can occur much more quickly.

The following pages provide supplemental resources that might enhance the preparation for the dedication and renewal of families. You will find several hymns, readings, stories and theological reflections, and a seasonal prayer. May these resources become a seasoning to add new flavor to this important celebration. May you experience new imaginations, insights, and actions.

# Come to Me, My Little Children

**Claude Douglas Bryan**

**Suggested Tunes:** NETTLETON
HOLY MANNA
BEECHER
Meter: 8.7.8.7.D.

Come to me, my little children,
Jesus spoke so long ago.
You are welcome in God's Garden,
All who live with Christ in love.
Matters not our age or wisdom,
We are little children still,
Always needing words of comfort
Healing hurts from each new day.

Thank thee, Lord, for sacred prunings
When our choices lead from thee;
Prone to follow inclinations,
Whose deceptions lead to harm.
Sunlight breaks through clouds of darkness,
Showing paths that we should take;
Lead us in the homeward journey
With thy word to guide our will.

Blest are we by Living Water,
Growing stronger through the years.
Tend our roots throughout the seasons;
May thy fruit become mature;
May we stray not from the Garden
And the One who waits for us;
As we bring home rocks and flowers,
We are never turned away.

# Guard This Child

**Claude Douglas Bryan**                        **Suggested Tunes: ALETTA**
**VIENNA**
**GOTT SEI DANK DURCH ALLE**
**Meter: 7.7.7.7.**

Praise we sing for life anew!
Hope shines through this sleeping smile,
Brought in love because of You.
God renews us all the while.

Bless the lives who stand here now!
Give them courage for their task,
Finding ways that will allow
Light and love from God, we ask.

Give us wisdom now to guide,
Showing them Incarnate care,
Teaching them in God to bide.
Life for service, we prepare.

Nurture each in time and place.
Help each stand as now we do,
When they call upon thy grace—
Living love that flows from You.

# Guard This Child (with refrain)

**Claude Douglas Bryan**

**Suggested Tune: CHINA**
**Meter: 7.7.7.7. with Refrain**

Praise we sing for life anew!
Hope shines through this sleeping
  smile,
Brought in love because of You.
God renews us all the while.
Let faith beam daily,
Let hope flow freely,
Let love glow clearly,
Let Kingdom life begin!

Bless the lives who stand here now!
Give them courage for their task,
Finding ways that will allow
Light and love from God, we ask.
Let faith beam daily,
Let hope flow freely,
Let love glow clearly,
Let Kingdom life begin!

Give us wisdom now to guide,
Showing them Incarnate care,
Teaching them in God to bide.
Life for service, we prepare.
Let faith beam daily,
Let hope flow freely,
Let love glow clearly,
Let Kingdom life begin!

Nurture each in time and place.
Help each stand as now we do,
When they call upon thy grace—
Living love that flows from you.
Let faith beam daily,
Let hope flow freely,
Let love glow clearly,
Let Kingdom life begin!

# Homes Are Where Our Loved Ones Dwell

**Claude Douglas Bryan**

**Suggested Tunes: ALETTA
GOTT SEI DANK DURCH ALLE WELT
Meter: 7.7.7.7.**

Homes are where our loved ones dwell;
Roots from God help us excel.
Love from God, we gladly tell.
Rich or poor, our life is well.

Homes are havens where we go,
Finding God we hope to know;
Love received helps each one grow,
Love to others we might show.

Homes through God can transform hearts;
Broken lives can know new starts.
Learning how to live our parts,
Homes teach heaven's holy arts.

Homes become God's healing place,
Burdens shared, may grace erase;
Strength from others helps to face—
Needs and hurts from daily pace.

# Families (Poem)

Families
Not easy to define?
How many needed?
As few as two?
What about the one?
Extended or immediate?
Close and loving?
Distant and indifferent?
Roles and rules?
Enmeshment or boundaries?
Opened or closed?
Life giving or life stealing?
Inward or outward?

Not easy to define,
Both genders needed?
Biological or spiritual?
Powerful and influencing?
New through rebirth?
Old through birth?
Common purpose?
Common goals?
Responsible or irresponsible?
Restrictive or nonrestrictive?
Caring or controlling? Not easy to define!

## Questions to Ponder

1. How would you describe the concept of family?
2. What does being a member of a family require?
3. Is the local community of faith a family?
4. What responsibilities do members of a faith community have to each other?

 

## Being Family (Responsive Reading)

LEADER: We are called to be God's people, one family, brothers and sisters to one another. Jesus said, "For whosoever shall do the will of my Father which is in heaven, the same is my brother, and sister, and mother" (Matthew 12:50). One family, brothers and sisters.

PEOPLE: One family, brothers and sisters.

LEADER: How do we build the family?

PEOPLE: "Except the LORD build the house, they labour in vain that build it: except the LORD keep the city, the watchman waketh but in vain" (Psalm 127:1).

LEADER: How do we build the house, the family?

PEOPLE: "…But as for me and my house, we will serve the LORD" (Joshua 24:15).

LEADER: We must choose whom we will serve. We serve as one called by God. What do we owe one another?

PEOPLE: "Owe no man any thing, but to love one another: for he that loveth another hath fulfilled the law" (Romans 13:8).

LEADER: Love is both our responsibility and privilege. This type of love is love in actions sensitive to the needs of others.

PEOPLE: "Be kindly affectioned one to another with brotherly love: in honour preferring one another" (Romans 12:10).

LEADER: What does the Lord say we should give to one another?

PEOPLE: "Submitting yourselves one to another in the fear of God" (Ephesians 5:21).

LEADER: What should be a characteristic behavior of our church family?

**PEOPLE:** "Be of the same mind one toward another. Mind not high things, but condescend to men of low estate. Be not wise in your own conceits" (Romans 12:16).

**PEOPLE:** How should we treat those in need?

**PEOPLE:** "But if any provide not for his own and specially for those of his own house, he hath denied the faith, and is worse than the infidel" (1 Timothy 5:8).

**LEADER:** What should we encourage in one another?

**PEOPLE:** "And let us consider one another to provoke unto love and to good works: not forsaking the assembling of ourselves as the manner of some is, but exhorting one another: and so much the more, as ye see the day approaching" (Hebrews 10:24-25).

**LEADER:** How are we to treat those new to our family?

**PEOPLE:** "Now therefore ye are no more strangers and foreigners, but fellow citizens with the saints, and of the household of God" (Ephesians 2:19).

**LEADER:** What shall we as a church body pursue?

**PEOPLE:** "Let us therefore follow after the things which make for peace, and things wherewith one may edify another" (Romans 14:19).

**LEADER:** "BEHOLD, how good and how pleasant it is for brethren to dwell together in unity!" (Psalm 133:1)

**PEOPLE:** Together in unity.

*ALL:* Together in unity. Amen.

 

## Puzzling Puzzles

Recently for my birthday my son, Matthew, gave me a 1000-piece puzzle depicting an antique shop. To Matthew's credit, he did consult with his mother about the appropriateness of the puzzle. My wife thought it was a great idea and agreed to help in putting the puzzle together.

One-thousand pieces? I imagine that a 500-piece puzzle would be sufficiently challenging. However, this gift was the puzzle that I was given. We began by compiling the pieces with a straight edge. From this pile of pieces with straight edges, we began constructing the border. The process continued with gathering pieces with a common color or design and then searching for the right fit.

Creating family is like putting together a puzzle. We have an idea what our family should look like. The idea and the reality may not perfectly coincide. The product is constantly changing and may or may not be what we originally thought. In a puzzle, we know what the finished product should resemble. A picture of the puzzle guides the process. In life, we do not know what the family will look like. Each puzzle piece fits in a manufactured design; people are more complex than puzzle pieces. Rather than a static and identifiable puzzle piece, each person is dynamic, sometimes growing smaller or larger, sometimes the edges changing their configuration. Roles, expectations, experiences, temperaments, maturations, and talents impact the individual and the family. The challenge is to create harmony and keep the family together in a way that encourages each member to grow in their own uniqueness while staying connected.

In the end, we know what the puzzle will be; in the end, the family may or may not be what we imagined. The whole is greater than the sum of its individual parts. Like families, the Kingdom of God shares these qualities. What we realize is beyond what we imagined.

## Questions to Ponder

1. In what other ways could you compare families with puzzles?
2. What lessons from putting together a puzzle could apply to rearing a family?
3. Can the discussion of and construction of a puzzle be a means of communicating the Gospel? If so, explain.

## The Masked and the Unmasked

In the best of worlds, each local church body is family. We are brothers and sisters to one another. In missionary circles, appointed missionary adults are the aunts and uncles to the children of their colleagues. These nieces and nephews are often close to one another, although I am not sure if they regard each other as cousins. It is not uncommon for these "cousins" to form marriages.

While we may not be missionaries on a foreign field who form relationships when original familial relationships are not physically possible, this practice has significance for the church. Do we treat each other as though we are family to one another? Scripture describes the early church as brothers and sisters to one another.

Not all families or churches are united. Paul addresses the church at Corinth who had fallen to the temptations of divisions. Brothers and sisters identified themselves as being of Apollos, of Paul, and of Peter, etc. While there may not be intended political or theological positions, they do indicate a difference in loyalty to teachings and traditions. These alliances disrupted harmony and the unity of the church.

As I write, we are in a continuing pandemic caused by the COVID-19 virus. Churches have responded in numerous ways, as have individuals. There are those who deny the virus, who question the vaccine, who regard the pandemic as political, and who refuse to wear a mask. Whatever the reason or the position, an unprecedented division has become apparent.

I have been part of a church that tragically experienced the division brought to the surface by the pandemic. While we were able to maintain unity despite diversity in political positions, ranges of wealth, and native-born versus outsiders, the unity dissolved. We became self-labeled into pro-mask and anti-mask groups.

The book of the Revelation of Saint John the Divine describes a church who lost her first love. When I first read those words, I did not understand the implications behind that observation. Lost love for Christ shows itself in lost love for one another; lost love impacts how we regard and respect one another; and lost love diminishes respect and the worth of others.

 

## Questions to Ponder

1. Have you observed disharmony in local churches?

2. How open is the church to the stranger, the outsider?

3. How can old and new members be harmonized into one family?

4. What have you learned about yourself or your church during the pandemic?

# God of Families

God of families, both large and small, we gather today acknowledging that you are the parent of all. Just as the child must listen to the parents, may we each listen to your admonitions this day. Help us to see the family of God as ever growing. Remove us from our isolation and into communities of faith where we are bound together by love, commitment, and openness to the presence of others. Help us to renew our commitment to one another so that we may find the ability to invite others to share in that commitment. Assist us to be extended family both to those we know and to those we have yet to know.

Forgive us when we fail one another to live as one family. We confess to you our tendencies to self-absorption, self-centeredness, and self-involvement to the neglect of others in need of grace. Renew us as a community of believers dedicated to finding the best for all your creation. May we not ask the questions of who is our neighbor or who is our family. Rather than narrow definitions and limited responsibilities, may we know the fullness of your measures of love. Provide light into our darkened understandings and light to our unknown paths this day. Thank you for allowing all to be a part of the kingdom. May the witnesses of the past encourage our living in greater love. May our brothers and sisters of the future find legacy markers to our faithfulness in having followed you. In the name of Jesus the Christ, we pray. Amen.

# TIMES OF GRADUATION

*Let no man despise thy youth; but be thou an example of the believers, in word, in conversation, in charity, in spirit, in faith, in purity.*
—1 Timothy 4:12

*Intelligence plus character—that is the goal of true education.*
—Martin Luther King Jr., *The Papers of Martin Luther King, Jr*

*Knowledge without wisdom is like water in the sand.*
—African Proverb

Graduation is viewed as a final celebratory exercise for an academic achievement, but in fact, graduation is only the beginning a new set of life's possibilities and responsibilities. Often it results in a degree, a diploma, or a certificate. However, graduations may also occur at the conclusion of other significant learning events or achievements. An important question is, what did the individual learn from the experience? Are there new skills, knowledge, ideas, or commitments? When I concluded my first full-time teaching assignment, a two-year missionary appointment in Nigeria, I reflected on my major takeaways. In Switzerland I purchased four shadow-box-size brass items to symbolize my values and commitments.

My items were two candlesticks to represent my commitment to be a person of light who shared both Gospel and learning; scales to present the need for fairness, accuracy, and justice for all; a mortar and pestle to represent the need to be a person of healing and mercy; and the globe to represent the importance of having a worldwide perspective and to being a world Christian, not a provincial one. Ironically, the globe broke from its stand. Soon I discovered the hidden accidental message and meaning. We live in a broken world. These were my graduation takeaways from my teaching assignment.

Celebrate within congregational life the graduation moments of individuals or groups, not as a simple event or achievement, but as a memorable declaration of learning and commitment.

The following pages provide resources that might enhance the preparation for the celebration of graduation. You will find several hymns, readings, stories and theological reflections, and a seasonal prayer. May these resources become a seasoning to add new flavor to this important celebration. May you experience new imaginations, insights, and actions.

                                                  

# We Sing This Day of Gladness

**Claude Douglas Bryan**                    **Suggested Tune: LANCASHIRE**
                                            **Meter: 7.6.7.6.D.**

We sing this day of gladness:
Their time of study done,
Our students shall move forward
To God's alluring sun.
From birth through life we watched them,
And ever proud are we.
God bless their life and movements
To places filled with thee.

O Lord, for years shall pass soon,
Too quickly we recall,
To them give visions guiding
In ways both great and small.
May they view each as God's own
To serve and love with joy;
To bring to God their gifts best
That life may all enjoy.

Keep lives and hearts anew filled
With thoughts both true and wise.
Good minds with hearts provide care
Where human needs arise.
For future tasks encourage
That others may stand tall.
Give faith and hope for their day,
Pursuing God's own call.

# God of Heaven, God of Earth

**Claude Douglas Bryan**

**Suggested Tunes:**
**ABERYSTWYTH**
**HERRNHUT**
**ORIENTIS PARTIBUS**
Meter: 7.7.7.7.

God of heaven, God of earth,
Offers all who come new birth.
Through the Christ we find new life,
Free from war and free from strife.
Lord, help these to find their place;
Service deeds may they embrace.
Finding wrongs may they amend,
Showing mercy has no end.

Humbleness we hope for each;
Open hearts to what you teach.
Various they are, linked by love,
Shine like heaven found above.
Keep them safe from evil's harm,
Close within your tender care.
Faith and trust needs no alarm,
Shows life lived through Christ most fair.

 

# God of Heaven, God of Earth (with refrain)

**Claude Douglas Bryan**                               **Suggested Tune: DIX**
**Meter: 7.7.7.7. with refrain**

God of heaven, God of earth,
Offers all who come new birth,
Through the Christ we find new life,
Free from war and free from strife.
May they show God's work today,
Follow Christ in ev'ry way.

Lord, help these to find their place;
Service deeds may they embrace.
Finding wrongs may they amend,
Showing mercy has no end.
May they show God's work today,
Follow Christ in ev'ry way.

Humbleness we hope for each;
Open hearts to what you teach.
Various they are, linked by love,
Shine like heaven found above.
May they show God's work today,
Follow Christ in ev'ry way.

Keep them safe from evil's harm,
Close within your tender care.
Faith and trust needs no alarm,
Shows life lived through Christ most fair.
May they show God's work today,
Follow Christ in ev'ry way.

# Graduation (Responsive Reading)

LEADER: Today is a day of anticipation as we honor these graduates and their families and friends. We celebrate their accomplishments. Some of you have been with us since your birth, and others have joined our community in your childhood years and others in your teens. To each we say, you are a part of our body in our thoughts and affections.

**PEOPLE:** You have been, you are, and you will continue to be a part of this body.

LEADER: The Apostle Paul describes the body as having many parts with differing functions and of equal value. You each have different sets of characteristics and abilities. You are gifted in multiple ways of intellect, in multiple ways of emotional intelligence, in multiple ways of social skills, and in multiple ways of physical skills. You are uniquely created, but you are part of one body.

**PEOPLE:** You have been, you are, and you will continue to be part of this body.

LEADER: You each have different immediate and long-term plans. Some will stay within this community, and others will travel to another part of the world. Some we will see daily and others not so often. But you are a part of us in the days ahead.

**PEOPLE:** You have been, you are, and you will continue to be a part of this body.

LEADER: With your graduations come the challenge to use what you have learned for the benefit of others and service to others. May you take the best of Christian faith and community with you. Will you do so?

*GRADUATES:* We will through God's mercy and grace.

LEADERSHIP: Go and share in this new world that belongs to you. Do not forget the family and church that have sought to love and to guide you. Forgive us for any mistakes me made.

*GRADUATES:* We give thanks to all who have loved us and have taught us.

LEADERSHIP: Remember the Lord your God.

*GRADUATES:* We will remember the Lord our God.

PEOPLE: May the Lord bless and keep you. Amen.

     

# Mixed Feelings, Easily Shaken (Poem)

Mixed feelings, easily shaken
Hopes and fears
Last-minute details, nightmares of incomplete work
Looking back and looking ahead
No longer a senior
Now an alum
Places gained
Places lost
Starting over
Unclear plans
Top of the food chain
Bottom of the food chain
Starting over
Regrets and accomplishments
Unfamiliar, now familiar
Saying goodbyes
New introductions
Firsts never the same
What's next
Mixed feelings, easily shaken

## Questions to Ponder

1. What are some common fears among graduates or soon-to-be graduates?
2. What role, if any, should the community of faith have toward graduates?
Explain.
3. How can the faith of these graduates be strengthened in their transition?

## Homework and Witness

The baccalaureate sermon was about homework. In her closing remarks to the high school and college graduates, the pastor told the following story: Many details of her freshman year eluded my friend. Having only known what it meant to be consciously growing as a Christian for four months, she was overwhelmed. She was in a freshman ancient history survey with a demanding thirty-something-year-old professor of German nationality.

Once the professor spoke about his upbringing in World War II. As best she recalled, he said there was a photograph of him as a young child on Hitler's knee. As a youth, he attended a religious crusade in his native Germany. Very solemnly, the professor recalled that he had been "moved" during the message. During the time of the "invitation," the professor stepped forward. He recalled how he was given a tract with cartoon-like depictions of statements on the Christian life. His tone of voice reiterated how he wanted much more than the simple cartoon-like tract in answer to his deep questions. He went away saddened, it seemed, by the experience.

My friend did not know how to respond to the disappointment she sensed behind her professor's professional demeanor. She only could read her assignments and participate in class discussion. The professor came to identify her in class as one who would answer questions. On occasion, he would ask for her responses as a Christian to a historical theme found in Plato's *The Republic*. Looking back, she thought she must have sounded immature. Feeling as though she represented the voice of Christianity was uncomfortable, but she noticed that the professor seemed to have a softer and more respectful tone toward her.

As she told the story, she didn't know what happened to her ancient history teacher. Did he ever find deeper answers to his questions?

Outcomes of our witness often remain a mystery. The pastor closed by sharing that by doing our homework, we are not impediments to someone's listening to the Gospel message.

### Questions to Ponder

1. Do we all have homework that we might do?
2. Could doing our homework impact the credibility of what we say and what we do?

 

# Cruising and Changing

Cruises can be challenging and life changing. My wife and I tested the cruise waters with a five-day cruise. Now one of my favorite vacation endeavors is going on a cruise. Simply stated, I love cruising. I enjoy what I consider to be an economical way to vacation with its all-inclusive package. I don't regard it as a floating petri dish, as I once heard a science professor friend describe it. Some cruise devotees will take a cruise anywhere; the cruising is more important than the destinations. In my experience, the sights and sounds provide a chance to relax, to renew, to reflect, to review, to rest, and, of course, to eat.

One of the more famous cruises for those with missionary interests is the cruise of Adoniram Judson, Ann Haseltine Judson, and Luther Rice. In 1812, these three were part of a missionary party traveling around the world to a place called Burma. Rather than engaging in casino gambling, folding towels into animals, and answering trivia questions, all very common in today's cruise adventures, these three Congregationalist missionaries engaged in a Bible study. As they studied the Greek New Testament, they gradually came to new conclusions and convictions about believer's baptism by immersion. The three were rebaptized by immersion by a Baptist missionary. The three, no longer Congregationalist missionaries with church support, were now three Baptists without church support. Luther Rice would return to the United States, traveling the Eastern Seaboard to inform and request support for the Judsons as Baptist missionaries. The Judsons would spend forty years in Burma (present-day Myanmar) in missionary endeavors. Rice would participate in creating and supporting a missionary-sending body of Baptists.

These three were changed by a cruise and biblical study. Cruising can be a metaphor for the journey for graduates. Expectations of destinations and careers may be clear or unclear. Like the Judsons and Rice, those on the journey may be changed by what they learn on the way. The journey is important, if not more than the destination.

## Questions to Ponder

1. Which is more important, the ends or the means? Explain.
2. How have you changed since your own graduation?
3. What would you say to today's graduates?

# God of Learning and Teaching

God of learning and teaching, look favorably upon each of us this day. We come to celebrate the accomplishment of these graduates [add the names of the graduates] who have studied and worked toward this day. We call this day a day of commencement, and truly it is a day to commence in new endeavors, comments, and challenges. Give them time for celebration, for shared remembrances of a journey, and for thankfulness for teachers and others who made this day possible. Help each to see today as the beginning and a continuation of life in service.

Be with these graduates, their families, and their friends in honoring what this day signifies. Bless those who continue further study; bless those who will enter the full-time workforce. May what has been learned be transformed into new creativity and productivity. We study for a purpose; we live for a Savior with our heads and our hearts for service. Protect them in the days ahead with new expectations and new responsibilities. Thank you for allowing us to be a part of their journey. Should their journey allow them to remain with us, we are grateful; should their journey take them away, we are grateful, as well. Let them live lives of honor and purpose in your Kingdom. Let us remember the small roles that we as a congregation have played in their lives. Forgive us when we may have failed them. Show us how to encourage them more. May the time come when we are joined together in perfect harmony and peace. In the name of Jesus the Crucified, we pray. Amen.

# TIMES OF HISTORICAL REMEMBRANCE

*He hath made his wonderful works to be remembered:
the LORD is gracious and full of compassion.*
—Psalm 111:4

*What is past is prologue.*
—William Shakespeare

*Prove that you understand the worth of time by employing it.*
—Louisa May Alcott

One of the topics that has captivated human thought and imagination is understanding what it means to be created in the image of God. While I would not presume that I could bring a comprehensive understanding of this beautiful phrase, "the image of God," I would offer that one quality of human beings is the ability to remember and the power of remembering.

Developmental psychology teaches that human memory begins with the infant's acquiring object permanence—the ability to know that objects exist even when out of his or her visual field. Thus, we set in motion the ability to remember.

Transmission of one set of information, attitudes, and values from one generation to the next involves the process of remembering. While we have individual memory, we also have memory that emerges from our cultural group. At the end of life, perhaps, the greatest pain involves losing our memory. We may forget the past, distort the past, or fail to relive the moments. We may lose our identity that connects the experiences and relationships we have encountered across the lifespan.

Church is a time to remember. We seek to remember noteworthy events in human history and our individual history. It involves elaborating on those milestones. We might remember when we first professed faith, denominational heritage, a marriage date, a graduation, or a death. Collectively we remember the celebration of a minister's tenure at church, the anniversary of a church building, or the works of mission endeavors.

Ceremonial remembering binds us to one another in community. Look for ways to appropriately celebrate the past, but let the past be the fuel for the future. If we fail to retell, we soon will forget. Distinct types of exile call for an opportunity to remember, lest we forget.

The following pages provide supplemental resources that might enhance the preparation for remembering important events. You will find several hymns, readings, stories and theological reflections, and a seasonal prayer. May these resources become a seasoning to add new flavor to this important celebration. May you experience new imaginations, insights, and actions.

 

# Candles of Witness

**Claude Douglas Bryan**                    **Suggested Tune: SLANE**
**Meter: 10.10.10.10.**

Born near the mountains and miles from the sea,
Settlers first worshipped by water and tree,
Leaving forever their fam'ly and home,
Building and serving a church of their own.

Times of plenty and times of need,
Working together and seeking thy lead;
Facing the future and trusting thy grace;
Caring for all that our Lord would embrace.

Growing in numbers and seeking thy light;
Learning to live as one under God's sight;
Sending out loved ones to share in God's love;
Helping each other to know life above.

Sharing and living redemption's great call;
Building the body, still open to all;
Places of worship designed by God's light—
Candles of witness by day and by night.

Make us your candles still showing the Way,
Melted and molded, God's love we obey;
May we your church be born daily, we pray—
True to Christ who keeps us safe, lest we stray.

# Join These Moments We Remember

**Claude Douglas Bryan**

**Suggested Tunes: HOLY MANNA
BEACH SPRING
WYCLIFF
STUTTGART
Meter: 8.7.8.7.D.**

Join these moments we remember
What transpired in passing days,
What we shared in faith together,
Onward changed in newfound ways.

Memories remain in these days;
May your presence bring new joy.
Hopeful power gives renewed blaze;
Truth and grace we shall enjoy.

Praise to God in joys and sorrows;
Heaven gives its comfort clear.
Work our days and our tomorrows;
God's love reigns both far and near.

Praise to Grace who moves us onward;
Bless this time and bless our place;
Clear our paths to guide us Son ward;
Past with hope for future's face.

# Recorded Events (Poem)

Recorded events and explanations,
Captured by one's perspective;
Told and retold,
Layered with meaning,
Covering and guiding our memory,
Shaping ideas and actions.

Vital to be recorded,
Lest forgotten;
Witnesses needed
To tell the story;
Lives not totally lost,
Remembered for
What they were;
Remembered for
What might have been.

Always changing
With new ideas;
Shaping the past
Into ways more pleasant;
Claiming simple understanding;
Life never simple, always complex,
Recorded and revealed
Into complex ways to understand.

## Questions to Ponder

1. What was the importance of remembering to the Hebrews?
2. What role does remembering play today for Christians?
3. What should be remembered within your community of faith?
4. What should you as an individual remember with the passing of each year?

# To Everything (Responsive Reading)

SPEAKER 1: "To every thing there is a season, and a time to every purpose under the heaven" (Ecclesiastes 3:1).

**SPEAKER** 2: "For I know the thoughts that I think toward you, saith the LORD, thoughts of peace, and not of evil, to give you an expected end" (Jeremiah 29:11).

SPEAKER 1: "A time to be born, and a time to die" (Ecclesiastes 3:2a).

*SPEAKER* 3: "For we are his workmanship, created in Christ Jesus unto good works, which God hath before ordained that we should walk in them" (Ephesians 2:10). "For whether we live, we live unto the Lord; whether we die, we die unto the Lord: whether we live therefore, or die, we are the Lord's" (Romans 14:8).

SPEAKER 1: "A time to plant, and a time to pluck up that which is planted" (Ecclesiastes 3:2b).

**SPEAKER** 2: "He causeth the grass to grow for the cattle, and herb for the service of man: that he may bring forth food out of the earth" (Psalms 104:14). "Yea, the LORD shall give that which is good; and our land shall yield her increase" (Psalm 85:12).

SPEAKER 1: "A time to kill, and a time to heal" (Ecclesiastes 3:3a).

*SPEAKER* 3: "Whoso sheddeth man's blood, by man shall his blood be shed: for in the image of God made he man" (Genesis 9:6). "He healeth the broken in heart, and bindeth up their wounds" (Psalm 147:3).

SPEAKER 1: "A time to break down, and a time to build up" (Ecclesiastes 3:3b).

**SPEAKER** 2: "See, I have this day set thee over the nations and over the kingdoms, to root out, and to pull down, and to destroy, and to throw down, to build, and to plant" (Jeremiah 1:10).

SPEAKER 1: "A time to weep, and a time to laugh" (Ecclesiastes 3:4a).

 

*SPEAKER* 3: "My face is foul with weeping, and on my eyelids is the shadow of death" (Job 16:16). "Then was our mouth filled with laughter, and our tongue with singing: then said they among the heathen, The LORD hath done great things for them" (Psalm 126:2).

SPEAKER 1: "A time to mourn, and a time to dance" (Ecclesiastes 3:4b).

**SPEAKER** 2: "And in that day did the Lord GOD of hosts call to weeping, and to mourning, and to baldness, and to girding with sackcloth" (Isaiah 22:12). "Thou hast turned for me my mourning into dancing: thou hast put off my sackcloth, and girded me with gladness" (Psalm 30:11).

SPEAKER 1: "A time to cast away stones, and a time to gather stones together" (Ecclesiastes 3:5a).

*SPEAKER* 3: "Seeing his days are determined, the number of his months are with thee, thou hast appointed his bounds that he cannot pass" (Job 14:5).

SPEAKER 1: "A time to embrace, and a time to refrain from embracing" (Ecclesiastes 3:5b).

**SPEAKER** 2: "And if ye salute your brethren only, what do ye more than others? Do not even the publicans so?" (Matthew 5:47)

SPEAKER 1: "A time to get, and a time to lose" (Ecclesiastes 3:6a).

*SPEAKER* 3: "But lay up for yourselves treasures in heaven, where neither moth nor rust doth corrupt, and where thieves do not break through nor steal" (Matthew 6:20). "Sell that ye have, and give alms; provide yourselves bags which wax not old, a treasure in the heavens that faileth not, where no thief approacheth, neither moth corrupteth. For where your treasure is, there will your heart be also" (Luke 12:33-34).

SPEAKER 1: "A time to keep, and a time to cast away" (Ecclesiastes 3:6b).

**SPEAKER** 2: "She is a tree of life to them that lay hold upon her: and happy is every one that retaineth her" (Proverbs 3:18).

SPEAKER 1: "A time to rend, and a time to sew" (Ecclesiastes 3:7a).

*SPEAKER* 3: "And rend your heart, and not your garments, and turn unto the LORD your God: for he is gracious and merciful, slow to anger, and of great kindness, and repenteth him of the evil" (Joel 2:13). "No man also seweth a piece of new cloth on an old garment: else the new piece that filled it up taketh away from the old, and the rent is made worse" (Mark 2:21).

SPEAKER 1: "A time to keep silence, and a time to speak" (Ecclesiastes 3:7b).

**SPEAKER** 2: "And beholding the man which was healed standing with them, they could say nothing against it" (Acts 4:14). "O give thanks unto the LORD; call upon his name: make known his deeds among the people" (Psalm 105:1).

SPEAKER 1: "A time to love, and a time to hate" (Ecclesiastes 3:8a).

*SPEAKER* 3: "Let all your things be done with charity" (1 Corinthians 16:14). "The fear of the LORD is to hate evil: pride, and arrogancy, and the evil way, and the froward mouth, do I hate" (Proverbs 8:13).

SPEAKER 1: "A time of war, and a time of peace" (Ecclesiastes 3:8b).

**SPEAKER** 2: "And ye shall hear of wars and rumours of wars: see that ye be not troubled: for all these things must come to pass, but the end is not yet" (Matthew 24:6). "Follow peace with all men, and holiness, without which no man shall see the Lord" (Hebrews 12:14).

*ALL:* "To everything there is a season, and a time to every purpose under the heaven" (Ecclesiastes 3:1).

# Thrift Store

Only a few people knew of Emma Lou's secretly acquired ability. She could listen to the stories told and emotions held by inanimate objects. It might be a story from a discarded hairbrush, a red-handled kitchen serving spoon, an old manual typewriter lacking a ribbon, or even an unworn shirt still folded with pins.

Emma Lou had been in the homes and lives of the community for decades. She was known as a good listener, repeater, and communication expert. Emma Lou didn't miss much. Less friendly people might describe her as being a gossip rather than a spiritual listener and sharer.

Emma Lou volunteered at the neighborhood thrift store supported by donations to hospice. She learned that children did not always treasure the ordinary heirlooms of their parents. What had been precious to one was nothing special to another. Did they not know or did they not care? Households had to be cleaned out so that properties could be sold, she thought.

She handled merchandise carefully as she moved it from the donation carts to the shelves. As she touched each one, she felt that it told a story. A faded apron was the first garment a young girl had made in junior high school. She would go on and become a well-known seamstress in the community. This apron was the first, and she had set it aside for her children one day, but she failed to tell them the story.

The kitchen serving spoon had belonged to one man's mother, who carefully used it each time she made homemade soup. The serving spoon was all the woman left. The young son became a man and brought the serving spoon into his own family, but he failed to tell his children the history of the serving spoon. When he died, his own children and grandchildren donated the household items to the thrift store never knowing its story. Emma Lou became the only holder of the memories of the forgotten and discarded items. Was it by imagination, knowledge, or revelation?

## Questions to Ponder

1. What memories or information do you wish had been shared with you?
2. What memories or information do you need to share with others?
3. How well do you listen to the stories of others?

# Quick and Deadly

A few years ago I was part of the church committee tasked to lead fiftieth-anniversary celebrations of the construction of the current church building. Planning celebrations included a historical reenactment of the march down the street from the old church site to the new building site; special music from fifty years ago graced our worship service; worship participants included former staff members; greetings were shared from leaders in our denomination; and a dinner was served to all those attending. As a member of the committee, I learned about significant ministry events of the previous fifty years. I spent time researching old church bulletins, newsletters, and church minutes. I engaged in conversations with longtime church members. I wanted us to celebrate not the building itself but the ministry that occurred. We also took a special offering that went into a designated fund for community benevolence. While we were celebrating what had occurred, our focus was on future days and ministry opportunities.

The next year brought about a change in churches all over the world. We were in a pandemic, and face-to-face contacts were no longer safe options. Within several weeks, we had reexamined and adjusted office hours and established ways to maintain social distance. Sunday school classes took advantage of social media, and worship services were live-streamed. Our food pantry, our primary social ministry, continued to operate. While portions of the building were closed, church ministry continued. Offering opportunities were provided through a designed drop-off site and through online giving. We enjoyed a virtual choir. Pastoral visits were made on porch steps, in yards, and through email and telephone. A deacon ordination was conducted online. Deaf and grief ministries continued. We had the Lord's Supper online. We employed new church staff for vacant positions. Ministry continued.

And then the unforeseen and unthinkable occurred. We had a safety and protocol committee to create safety guidelines. With dissatisfaction over the realities of the pandemic, some did not want to follow safety protocol, refusing to wear masks and demanding that face-to-face worship occur. Harsh words and accusations were made. Recommendations from professional staff and specifically trained church members were ignored. Issues developed over who "owned" the church, with reminders of grandfathers and grandmothers who had built this church. The newcomers felt ignored; the older families felt ignored. It seemed that the least informed became the most vocal. We became a divided house. The demands continued that the church be reopened for ministry. Ministry had never ceased. Brought on by the pandemic, all of this happened within a few years following a wonderful celebration of the fiftieth anniversary of the church building. Was the church the building, or was the church the people?

## Questions to Ponder

1. Is this story familiar to you? Explain.
2. Can recognition and celebration of the past hinder the present and the future? Explain.
3. What are practical solutions for such dilemmas?

# God of the Past, Present, and Future

God of the Past, Present, and Future, God revealed in Jesus the Crucified, thank you for these moments of remembrance today. We recall many facts, faces, and memories as we commemorate [add the name of the event]. While it may appear simple to gather and to recall, we acknowledge that few things of importance come about easily without behind-the-scenes work, pain, disappointment, and uncertainty. We thank those who worked to make these moments possible. We are grateful for God's presence through all the phases of our planning. Help us today to remember those of the past, those present with us, and those future ones to come. May we learn to celebrate the best of these moments. May these moments energize us for the future, quiet us to moments of reflection, and call us to thanksgiving for your presence.

May the past, no matter how glorious and wonderful in our corporate memory, give us the encouragement to move forward in what is yet to be. Help us to share in the vision created by those long ago. May we provide our talents, our lives, our energy, and our resources in continuing the dreams started by people before us. May we learn from their victories and defeats; may those who come after us learn from our victories and defeats. Allow us to reflect on what we remember so that we might learn how to live with greater appreciation, attentiveness, and focus on your Kingdom. Let us come together as one during these moments. In the name of Jesus the Crucified, we pray. Amen.

# TIMES OF HOSPITALITY AND INVITATION

*Be not forgetful to entertain strangers:*
*for thereby some have entertained angels unawares.*
—Hebrews 13:2


*"That boy is your company.*
*And if he wants to eat up that tablecloth, you let him, you hear?"*
—Harper Lee, *To Kill a Mockingbird, Screenplay*


*The doors of churches, hotels, concert halls and reading rooms are alike closed*
*against the Negro as a man, but every place is open to him as a servant.*
—Ida B. Wells, *Crusade for Justice*

How do you invite or welcome others? Inviting others to hear and to participate in the Gospel is a form of evangelism. Evangelism is a word that causes many to become anxious. Rethinking evangelism and welcoming others to hear and to respond to the Gospel may be an alternative to viewing evangelism as an uncomplicated process or set of procedures.

At first glance, welcoming may mean how we say hello to others. Such spoken welcoming may involve the warmth of the voice, the placement of accent, and the gestures of the body. On a deeper level, the hello portion of the welcome is only the beginning toward genuine Christian hospitality. Rooted and sustained within Christian hospitality is the work and witness of God in Christ. There is much below the surface regarding the welcome. It is not just immediately what we see and what we feel at the scene; it is what goes on behind the scenes as well. Expressing genuine welcome is connected to the deepest levels of the individual and corporate heart.

Like hospitality, genuine and sustaining welcoming is a process and not one initial event. A familiar observation about church attrition is that as soon as they come in the front door, they exit from the back door. People come and depart because they may not have found the community engaging. Welcoming and hospitality must be continually nurtured. Welcoming and hospitality occur on many levels. There is an inquiring hospitality where honest answers are asked and diverse responses and thoughts are encouraged.

Recognizing the gifts of others, even when we might feel threatened, takes courage and confidence. A genuine gift of hospitality involves both the giving and the receiving of expressions of God's grace and work on the part of all. Hospitality involves offering a safe place of acceptance and nonjudgment. Within safety and belonging, we have the freedom and opportunity for authenticity to explore, to understand, and to express what it means to be created in the image of God. All persons have value. There cannot be second-class citizens in the Kingdom of God. If we have second-class citizens in the Kingdom, we do not have the real Kingdom. This equality means equal access to opportunities of ministry, of service, and of leadership at all levels. In hospitality, there cannot be glass ceilings, nor separate but equal policies. Full integration is the aspiration of genuine Christian community.

 

A good welcome, like a good introductory paragraph, provides an invitation to experience and to participate in the story of God's evolving community of grace. Demonstrating hospitality demands a great deal of energy and personal commitment on the part of the individual and the group.

The following pages provide supplemental resources that might enhance the preparation for observing and celebrating hospitality and invitation. You will find several hymns, readings, stories and theological reflections, and a seasonal prayer. May these resources become a seasoning to add new flavor to this important celebration. May you experience new imaginations, insights, and experiences.

# Welcome Lives

**Claude Douglas Bryan**

**Suggested Tune: TEMPUS ADEST FLORIDUM**
**Meter: 7.6.7.6. with Refrain**

Waiting in the crowds I watched,
Hoping out of sight;
Viewed and judged as one not washed,
Wanting change with all might.
Poor and hurting ones see clear,
Holy Spirit draw near;
Those who love and those who care
Welcome lives most dear.

Leave the crowds and search behind;
Longing hunger cease;
Hope and healing you will find;
Castaways find peace.
Poor and hurting ones see clear,
Holy Spirit draw near;
Those who love and those who care
Welcome lives most dear.

Seeking ones whose lives might shine,
Join the Father's welcome
Where both hearts and minds align;
Jesus bids us come.
Poor and hurting ones see clear,
Holy Spirit draw near;
Those who love and those who care
Welcome lives most dear.

# What a Joy

**Claude Douglas Bryan**

**Suggested Tunes:**
**GOTT SEI DANK DURCH ALLE WELT**
**SONG 13**
**Meter: 7.7.7.7.**

What a joy to follow Christ,
Finding life that sets us free;
Finding life becoming more
Than we thought first it could be.

Practicing agape love
Only shows what God can see;
Finding favor with God's plan,
Blessings both for you and me.

Harmony with faith and grace,
You and I are the new we.
Let true love reign; we are one,
Till our life and work is done.

## Hospitality (Catechism)

LEADER: "For I was an hungred, and ye gave me no meat: I was thirsty, and ye gave me no drink: I was a stranger, and ye took me not in: naked, and ye clothed me not: sick, and in prison, and ye visited me not" (Matthew 25:42-43).

PEOPLE: "…Lord, when saw we thee an hungred, or athirst, or a stranger, or naked, or sick, or in prison, and did not minister unto thee?" (Matthew 25:44)

LEADER: "Then shall he answer them, saying, Verily I say unto you, Inasmuch as ye did it not to one of the least of these, ye did it not to me" (Matthew 25:45).

PEOPLE: How are we to treat the disadvantaged?

LEADER: "Is it not to deal thy bread to the hungry, and that thou bring the poor that are cast out to thy house? when thou seest the naked, that thou cover him; and that thou hide not thyself from thine own flesh?" (Isaiah 58:7)

PEOPLE: What are we to pursue?

LEADER: "But a lover of hospitality, a lover of good men, sober, just, holy, temperate" (Titus 1:8).

PEOPLE: What should be our attitude?

LEADER: "And above all things have fervent charity among yourselves: for charity shall cover the multitude of sins. Use hospitality one to another without grudging" (1 Peter 4:8-9). "Be of the same mind one toward another" (Romans 12:16a). "If it be possible, as much as lieth in you, live peaceably with all men" (Romans 12:18).

PEOPLE: How are we to treat the alien?

LEADER: "And if a stranger sojourn with thee in your land, ye shall not vex him. But the stranger that dwelleth with you shall be unto you as one born among you, and thou shalt love him as thyself; for ye were strangers in the land of Egypt: I am the LORD your God" (Leviticus 19:33-34).

**PEOPLE:** How are we to treat fellow Christians?

**LEADER:** "Distributing to the necessity of saints; given to hospitality" (Romans 12:13).

**PEOPLE:** What must we remember?

**ALL:** "…Inasmuch as ye have done it unto one of the least of these my brethren, ye have done it unto me" (Matthew 25:40).

# Come (Invitational Reading)

We have worshipped the Creator God through our prayers, our readings, our praise, our music, and the preaching of God's word. We live in a broken and fallen world where all creation needs redemption. God has not abandoned his creation. Humans, created in God's image, have moments of failure.

God became human flesh and lived the life portrayed in the Gospels as Jesus the Christ. Jesus brought a message first to the Jewish people, and then disciples continued that message of acceptance to all people. Profound but simple, God loves all people, and God offers an open invitation to trust in him. God extends his grace but will not force commitment. By acknowledging our brokenness and by trusting in him who can heal, we become closer to God's intent for us.

We proclaim and extend God's invitation to you today. From God, a new life and new fellowship is offered to you today. We would welcome you to join the fellowship of God and to join us in living your life in this local community of faith. We are not perfect, but we are a body committed to become more Christ-like in our thinking, our attitudes, and our behavior. We invite you to join us. If you wish to accept this invitation or have questions, come forward during this invitation time. We will seek to guide you and support you as you share your concerns and questions. By God's grace, you will find a new home and a new family within this body. Come.

## Pack the Pew

Revival services were scheduled at the local church. One Friday evening was designated as "Pack the Pew Night." Participating church members were assigned a pew and encouraged to fill the pew with both church members and non-church members. The goal was for revival and new professions of faith. All should hear and respond to the message of the Gospel.

The young boy accepted the invitation and the call of the church to attend. He had only been involved in Sunday school and his parents were not involved at all. He and his mother went to the Friday night service. They entered the church, looking for a seat. The young boy went to a vacant pew and motioned for his mother to follow.

As they began to sit down, his mother said, "Something's wrong. I don't know that we're supposed to sit here."

Seeking to reassure her, the boy said to his mother, "It will be okay. Let's just sit."

Within moments, a man approached the mother and son. "Ma'am," he said, "you're sitting in my pew. This is the one that I've been assigned."

The mother and son arose. The mother said, "I'm sorry."

An older woman, hearing the interactions, approached the boy and his mother and said, "You can sit here with us. You can always sit on our pew."

The message of the sermon was not remembered by the boy, but he remembered not being able to sit at the original pew—an enduring impression on the young boy. It was his first attendance at a worship service, and he had asked his mother to accompany him. He and his mother never returned to the worship services of that church.

## Questions to Ponder

1. How powerful can first messages about the church be?
2. What is the power of invitation to Christian community?
3. Is invitation a one-moment experience?

# No Parking

Numerous tales are told and retold, not around inviting campfires but at any gathering of two or more at the watercooler, the office, the lunchroom, or the grocery aisles, regarding deacons' meetings. In my tradition of the last fifty years, deacons are the elected lay leadership. They are the elected servants of the church, though in some places their roles have more emphasis on leadership than servanthood.

Deacon discussions do not involve high intellectual engagement on such topics as the nature of the Lord's Supper, the merits of Calvinism or Arminianism, or critical race theory and church organization. More amazing, the discussion does not always center on ways to minister to youth who no longer attend the church, to couples and families in crisis, or to widows with financial needs. Rather, the discussion centers on how much are we "running" in Sunday school—and for those unfamiliar with "how much did you 'run,'" it refers to attendees or numbers. Other familiar topics include the status of the air-conditioning system or the benefits of mulch or straw around the shrubs at the front of the church.

One of my vivid recollections is when our perennial discussions focused on how to make the church more appealing and attractive to visitors, such as changing our times of worship; adding screens to the auditorium or the sanctuary, depending on your theological vocabulary preference; and deciding whether to have more radio music and less high church music.

Suddenly, one deacon whose last name was also the last name of the town, declared, "What bothers me is when people park on the grass."

"What people?" someone asked.

"You know who I am talking about," the town's namesake said.

"No, I don't," said the deacon whose birth certificate indicated that he was not born in the county.

"I mean the university across the street. They've got cars and vans parked on our grass for the ball games," he said.

"They should park on the gravel, not the grass," another deacon said.

"What would you like for me to do about this?" the deacon chair asked.

"Talk to the university about the situation," some said.

"If that is the pleasure of the body, I will," the deacon chair said.

Most of the heads nodded in agreement.

     

"Maybe we should have a sign that says 'No Parking on the Grass,'" someone muttered. "Or maybe 'No Visitor Parking.'"

"I think that is something for the building and property committee to discuss and bring us a recommendation."

Agreeing heads nodded. The chair of the building and grounds committee agreed as well.

"Now, we need to return to last week about purchasing a large multimedia sign that welcomes the community," the deacon chair stated.

"Yeah, we need to let people know who we are," one deacon added.

## Questions to Ponder

1. Do our practices and processes welcome others into our church?
2. Did you find any surprises in the above imaginary glimpse into a meeting of church leadership?

# God of Hospitality and Invitation

God of hospitality and invitation, we give witness to the multiple invitations that you offer us, both now and in the future. Even though we are unworthy, you have counted us worthy of hospitality and invitation. When we were discouraged, you offered comfort; when our behavior was unacceptable, you offered cleansing; and when we were apathetic to your invitation, you gave us a chance once more to care.

Feed us today, Lord, so that we might feed others tomorrow. Give us acceptance so that we might accept others. Give us opportunity so that we might give others opportunity. May all the gifts we have be regarded as ones to be shared with others. May gifts of kindness not end with us but be demonstrated to all. Give us what we cannot give ourselves alone. Help us to be kind to the stranger; help us to be kind to those who disagree with us; help us to be kind to those who have wronged us; and help us to be kind to those who have harmed us. May we follow the example of Jesus the Christ, who went about doing good. In the name of Jesus the Crucified, the source of all hospitality and invitation, we pray. Amen.

# TIMES OF LENT

*Then said Jesus unto his disciples, If any man will come after me,
let him deny himself, and take up his cross, and follow me.*
—Matthew 16:24


*No act of virtue can be great if it is not followed by advantage for others.
So, no matter how much time you spend fasting, no matter how much you
sleep on a hard floor and eat ashes and sigh continually, if you do no good to
others, you do nothing great.*
—John Chrysostom


*Lenten fasts make me feel better, stronger, and more active than ever.*
—St. Catherine of Genoa

A misunderstood concept to many, Lent is a dedicated time to remember and to be changed by the power of God. In Lent we give up something of value to gain something of more value. As Advent prepares us for the observation of Christmas, Lent prepares us to understand and celebrate Easter. Both times of preparation lead us in a concerted effort of thinking and meditating on what it means to be a follower of Christ.

Lent is a time of preparation in which we focus our attention on the meaning of the elements of the birth narrative, the life and teaching of Jesus on earth, the events leading to the crucifixion, and the outcomes and message of the resurrection. In the beginning, God who becomes flesh and blood leads us to new birth on earth and continued life with God. It is a movement from the temporal to the eternal. We repeat and reenact this miraculous journey of life and redemption.

Beginning on Ash Wednesday and concluding the Saturday before Easter Sunday, Lent lasts for approximately forty days. Those churches celebrating Lent focus on fasting, praying, and almsgiving. Fasting involves giving up what gives us pleasure so our thoughts and attention may be focused more closely on Jesus the Christ. This observation seeks to bring us into closer intimacy with God eternal and to live out this redemptive message with our neighbor.

The following pages provide supplemental resources that might enhance the preparation for the celebration of Lent. You will find several hymns, readings, stories and theological reflections, and a seasonal prayer. May these resources become a seasoning to add new flavor to this important celebration. May you experience new imaginations, insights, and actions.

   

# Lent Makes Way for Celebration

**Claude Douglas Bryan**            **Suggested Tune: BEECHER**
**Meter: 8.7.8.7.D.**

Lent, the season, leads to Easter; forty preparation days;
Christians journey through the desert, walking steps in holy ways;
Opens hidden lives before God; true and honest we become;
Faith and trust renews our being; near and far to him we come.

Lead through self-examination, bringing darkness into light.
Help us work out our salvation; prick our hearts to be contrite.
Fasting helps us to remember—love of Christ transforms our ways.
Leaving what we hold most precious, God's fresh fullness fills our days.

Lent makes way for celebration; sorrows bow before God's might;
Easter's found for God's creation, through the day and through the night.
Lent brings thoughts of contemplation, looking deep within our strife.
Easter sings of resurrection, hope of every Christian life.

# May We Show Your Love Today

**Claude Douglas Bryan**

**Suggested Tunes: ALETTA
MONKLAND
GOTT SEI DANK DURCH
ALLE WELT
Meter: 7.7.7.7.**

May we show your love today,
Fearing not diversity,
Living free the Christ-like way,
Showing new humanity.

God of Truth and God of Grace,
Holy love we shall embrace;
Lord unite our human race;
Brother, Sister we embrace.

Give the Spirit of the One
Into lives that would be still;
Giving love in Christ has won;
Change our lives and hopes fulfill.

   

# What Is Lent? (Catechism)

LEADER: What does Lent literally mean?

**PEOPLE:** It means forty days.

LEADER: When does it begin and when does it end?

**PEOPLE:** Lent begins with Ash Wednesday and continues until Easter Sunday.

LEADER: What activities occur during Lent?

**PEOPLE:** It involves abstinence from some physical pleasure; it involves prayer; and it involves almsgiving or acts of kindness to those in need.

LEADER: Why do we abstain from some physical pleasure?

**PEOPLE:** We abstain to remember the sacrifices and life of Jesus the Christ on our behalf.

LEADER: Why do we focus on prayer?

**PEOPLE:** We focus on prayer to draw closer to God and to God's will for our lives. As we pray, we are instructed in godliness and holiness.

LEADER: Why do we engage in acts of kindness or almsgiving to the needy?

**PEOPLE:** We give alms to fulfill God's love for all people and to increase our love for those in need. Almsgiving allows us to share our practice of Lent with others.

LEADER: Is Lent essential for our salvation?

**PEOPLE:** Not for our salvation. Salvation is a gift of God's grace. Lent is a voluntary part of our ongoing discipleship. Discipleship is living the life of salvation.

ALL: May we all draw nearer to Jesus the Christ during this season.

# Judas Iscariot (Monologue)

My name is Judas. Judas Iscariot. Perhaps you're shocked that I would dare to stand before you. I'm a little surprised myself. I, too, was a part of the followers of Jesus. I was even in the inner circle—not the innermost circle of James, John, and Peter, but I was close with him, too. I was part of the twelve.

Most of you do not know my full story, only what you've read. Most of the details of my life have been lost to history, as most of the details of your life will be lost one day. In one or two generations, the details will be lost for most of us. Who can say? Join with me in my imagination.

I, too, was born into a Jewish family. I am not sure if we were wealthy or if we were poor. All I know is what I know—we got by. I grew up with the desire for the restoration of our nation. Some might claim that my family or extended family were bandits. I can't say. I did not like the Roman occupation of our sacred land. We belonged to no people other than to ourselves and to God. I was good at figures. I knew the worth behind silver. In fact, some of my family may have thought that I was too parsimonious with money. Only they used other words, not so nice.

I followed and listened to Jesus for three years. Three years of my life waiting for him to be acknowledged as the Messiah. Wandering across the Judean countryside providing and collecting money as needed. If there was a monetary need, they turned to me. I was important and valued. Not always trusted. Some people never trust those in charge of someone else's money. Money management can easily get you into trouble.

For three years, I followed Jesus. Not much, if any, of my activity was recorded, only the last episode. People try to look back and say that I was never truly a believer or follower. All I can say is that I followed him. Sure, I was puzzled and bothered by some of his teachings and demands. But aren't we all? Aren't you still puzzled and bothered by his teaching and his demands? Now, be honest.

I've heard that people sometimes refer to a "Judas kiss" as a sign of betrayal. Well, it makes it easier if they can blame me for the betrayal and find a flaw in my character. Perhaps it makes them feel safer, as though they are immune from betraying Jesus. Peter, now that guy was a braggart and quick tempered. Sometimes we forget that he betrayed Jesus as well. Well, let me say that you may be just like me, more than you are comfortable admitting. In fact, you are more like me than you can honestly admit in public. You could betray him just as I did. Sometimes, you may not even think of it as betrayal. You may think of quick ways to bring about the Kingdom of God. Perhaps you can set into motion a speedier intervention by God. Shortcuts have their own price to be paid. I should know.

You know about how I died. No need to recreate that story for you. Do have I regrets, you might ask. What do you think? There is a lingering question that some might ask. What would have happened if I had waited a few more days until I encountered the resurrected Jesus? Would he have forgiven me for my betrayal? Apparently, you know him better than I did. What do you think?

# Yard of the Month

When asked to described Lent, the pastor told her congregation about a young couple's dreams for a beautiful lawn.

The young couple had recently moved into the neighborhood, having bought the smallest house in the subdivision. Their inquisitive eyes scouted the neighborhood, looking for ideas on landscaping. What were the secrets of landscaping? One day they noticed the sign in the neighborhood with the designation "Yard of the Month," a prestigious award given in their small town.

The young couple waited until they saw the homeowner working in the yard. They approached her and introduced themselves.

"We noticed the award," the husband said.

"We're interested in seeking your advice," the young wife emphasized.

"Let's walk and I will talk about the plants," the homeowner said.

"Do you mind if we take notes?" the young wife asked.

"No, I don't mind," she replied.

She walked with the young couple, describing the details and design of her yard. They paused, the couple asking questions and taking notes. At the end of a discussion about trees, the homeowner described differences between annuals and perennials, shade-loving plants and sun-thriving plants, drought resistance, bloom times, types of soil, and issues of drainage. Soon it was obvious from her free and confident flow of information that she knew the requirements of those living plants on her lawn.

"You've learned a lot about gardening," the husband said.

"Gardening has taught me a lot about life, even my spiritual life."

"I don't understand," the young wife admitted.

"In the beginning, my husband and I planted plants, not according to the directions provided but according to our own ideas. Sometimes we planted too close together and discovered the plants could not thrive. We did not let in enough sunshine for the plants to grow tall and straight. Other times we gave too much water and at other times too little water. We failed to trim back some plants and pruned others too closely. We also spent much time digging up plants that were stunting the growth of other plants."

"Yes, but you eventually were awarded 'Yard of the Month'!"

 

"How long do you think it took us to gain the award?" the homeowner asked.

Silence.

"How long did it take?" the young wife asked.

"Ten years," the homeowner said, smiling. "But you know, the award came after we stopped thinking about outside recognition. We focused on what was best for our yard, and the award came later."

## Questions to Ponder

1. Are gardens a good metaphor for describing Lent? If so, what are the similarities?
2. Is there power in waiting?
3. What are your evaluations about the homeowner's last words in this story?
4. Is this story an appropriate one for Lent? Explain.

# Gaining by Giving Up

One of the basic messages of Western civilization is the desire for more. More land. More allegiance. More money. More opportunity. More power. More recognition. Acquiring more is everything. I was a sophomore in college when I first encountered *Through Gates of Splendor,* the missionary story of Jim Elliot written by his wife Elisabeth Elliot. One of the memorable lines is, "He is no fool who gives away what he cannot keep to gain what he cannot lose." Jim Elliot wrote these words in his spiritual journal. Perhaps the written thought was in response to those who questioned the talented young man who desired to spend his life among primitive tribes in South America. I copied Jim Elliot's sentence into the front pages of my green-padded *Living Bible.*

Giving up is not easy to do. I remember a fellow student who made the declaration that he was giving up sex for Lent. I thought his statement was serious until I learned that he was a single seminarian. Lent involves giving up something of value to draw us closer to Jesus the Christ and his atoning love. This discipline is a sacred and extensive experience for some Christian traditions and an unfamiliar practice for others. The reason for the discipline is not to deprive oneself as an end in itself. Instead, the practice calls our attention back to the love of God. Much like Jim Elliot, may we discern the great good that comes from giving up things of lesser importance. Lent calls us to know what is important and what has lesser value.

## Questions to Ponder

1. What are the potential values of observing Lent?
2. Do we measure the value of the time and energy invested in our interests? Explain.
3. When have you given up something for a greater good? Explain.

# God of the Resurrection

God of the resurrection of Jesus the Christ, we spend these moments reflecting and preparing to remember, to proclaim, and to celebrate your victory over death. Through this demonstrated love, we have new power and understanding of life today and life tomorrow. Jesus displayed a sacrificial servant life in which daily resurrection occurred, with the final resurrection on Easter morning. Evil could not triumph over Good. A life well lived was offered in community.

As children, we may have focused on the bounty of our own Easter baskets full of candies, treats, toys, and other brightly wrapped gifts. We have Easter egg hunts to determine who can accumulate the most eggs and who can find the most prized eggs. Easter egg hunts are for children and for adults who enjoy the joy of the children's chasing what they do not understand. Unfortunately and tragically, still today adults chase the elusive Easter eggs for their own benefit alone. We fight for the sweet life for ourselves and for our loved ones. We ignore those whose Easter baskets go unfilled.

God has provided the ultimate Easter basket filled with Acceptance, Love, and Resurrection. As adult believers, may we concentrate on the most precious gift of Easter, the life and love of the resurrected Jesus. Our brokenness and estrangement can be over through God's gift. Let us not concentrate on the candies and new outfits, unless we provide the candies and new outfits for all of God's children. May this message of Easter prepare us to live daily in remembrance and service. May we give up what we cannot keep to gain what we cannot lose (Jim Elliot). Following the One who gave all, in the name of Jesus the Crucified, we pray. Amen.

# TIMES OF MINISTRY APPRECIATION

*And I will give you pastors according to mine heart, which shall feed you with knowledge and understanding.*
—Jeremiah 3:15


*Many wise and true sermons are preached us every day by unconscious ministers in street, office or home; even a fair table may become a pulpit, if it can offer good and helpful words which are never out of season.*
—Louisa May Alcott


*The aching tooth is better out than in. To lose a rotting member is gain.*
—Richard Baxter

It did not take long before I realized the vulnerability of church staff members. My understanding began with words of criticism against the pastor. I do not recall the specifics of the criticism; however, I do remember the impression the words and the attitudes had on me. One comment does remain with me; one member said, "If Jesus Christ were the pastor, these people, whoever these people are, would say 'He works for us.'" Such a refrain or other equivalences are familiar in unsettled congregations.

I watched as the pastor, under increasing church criticism, remained silent. Jesus often remained silent to his critics. We have numerous instructions, conversations, and parables that Jesus told to increase knowledge and understanding and to change the hearts of those who would listen. Often, there were misunderstandings leaving the hearers confused and critical. Murmurings abounded.

Ministerial staff are often vulnerable to the whims of people within the congregation. While others may easily defend themselves when criticized, ministerial staff may be reluctant to engage in a battle of words. They must turn the other cheek and forgive in their desire to be Christ-like.

The church unfortunately is a place where people often vent their frustrations. Whether the frustration is in their personal life, their professional life, or their interpersonal life, the church might be a haven for the transference or projection of these feelings onto others. Their hurting remarks go unchallenged. They may not receive the feedback needed for correction and for growth. Unwarranted and non-redemptive criticism often goes unchallenged, leaving its victims to experience loneliness, frustration, and feelings of being unloved.

We must learn to strive for the same measures of acceptance and warmth that Jesus conveyed to his disciples. The command to come and follow me remains as clear today as it did two thousand years ago. Let us provide staff with extended acceptance, appreciation, and forgiveness, for they shepherd us. As we work together to achieve genuine Christian fellowship, let us shepherd one another.

The following pages provide supplemental resources that might enhance the preparation for celebrating the calling and appreciation of ministerial staff. You will find several hymns, readings, stories and theological reflections, and a seasonal prayer. May these resources become a seasoning to add new flavor to this important celebration. May you experience new imaginations, insights, and actions.

# Shepherds Seek the Lord's True Vision

**Claude Douglas Bryan**

**Suggested Tune:**
**TRYGGARE KAN INGEN VARA**
**Meter: 8.8.8.8.**

Shepherds seek the Lord's true vision,
Word spoken though our shepherds;
Keep us close to God's provision,
Proclamations true to God's Word.

Shepherds hear and follow God's call;
Lives of service show forgiveness;
Like them, placing God above all,
Loving others through our witness.

Keep our shepherds near your heart;
Bless their walking and their talking;
Changing them by heaven's sweet art;
Leading flocks beside Christ's way.

May we learn to say we thank you
Through our actions, through words spoken.
May we learn to say we love you,
Join their healing lives once broken.

## Young and Old Have Heard Your Call

**Claude Douglas Bryan**      **Suggested Tune:** ST. GEORGE'S WINDSOR
**Meter:** 7.7.7.7.D.

Young and old have heard your call,
Sometimes voices soft or loud;
Following has been their call;
Their devotion makes us proud.
Preparation they have done;
Study readies them to serve;
Work together we have won;
Work of God we shall preserve.

Calling claims their total life,
All submissions great and small;
Give away all forms of strife,
Seeking goodness for all.
Showing servants God-like care;
Words both sharp and hard are few;
Our support from God we share;
Working jointly is their due.

Thank you, Lord, for ones God-sent;
Servants show us each new day;
Giving best is their intent.
Help us share the Christ-like way.
Guide both life and afterlife;
Patience grant to all who serve;
Let our service live long life;
Trust and honors you deserve.

## Look and See (Poem)

Look around the room,
Look where the young ones are seated;
Their widened eyes are watching;
Their ears are listening;
Their senses understand emotions,
Summarizing what is going on in the room.

What are they observing in those who lead?
Is it always the same group?
The faithful twenty percent
Who are always present when
Doors are unlocked and the coffee is made—
Those who can be counted upon when the call is made.

What they know about us
Is what we have taught them;
Not through direct instruction but
Through modeling in words and actions.
They learn through observation and imitation;
Their play reveals our innermost selves.

## Questions to Ponder

1. What do the young learn from us in the way we treat ministerial leadership?
2. Who are your significant role models, both past and present, in the community of faith?
3. What have you learned from these role models?
4. What are we teaching our children by how we act both in and outside the church building? How can we improve?

## Ministry Appreciation (Responsive Reading)

LEADER: We thank you, Lord, that you call individuals to serve your people as we grow in Christian community under their leadership.

PEOPLE: Thank you for their calling.

LEADER: We thank you Lord for our staff [insert names] who serve as ministers for you and for his congregation.

PEOPLE: Thank you for [insert names of each staff member being recognized].

LEADER: We ask your richest blessings upon them, their families, their joint ministry, and their individual ministries.

PEOPLE: Give them your bountiful favor.

LEADER: May we provide support for their ministry.

PEOPLE: Provide support for their ministry.

LEADER: Forgive us for the failures we may have committed to them.

PEOPLE: Forgive us for our failures.

LEADER: Let us demonstrate appreciation and encouragement in words and actions both great and small.

PEOPLE: Demonstrate appreciation and encouragement.

LEADER: May our conversations become the language of building the body of Christ.

PEOPLE: Conversations that build the body of Christ.

LEADER: Let us learn to show forgiveness as we ask for forgiveness.

PEOPLE: Show forgiveness as we seek forgiveness.

LEADER: May we bring out the best of each of these ministers,

PEOPLE: As they seek to bring out the best in each of us.

*ALL:* May this community of faith grow together. Amen.

# The Chosen Ones

He was an ordinary high school graduate who had begun to display some academic achievement in the latter two years of high school. The growing achievement of those last two years did not compensate for the mediocrity of the first two years. He had no overt recognizable talent that would make him stand out in the crowd, as he would say. He was one who might be pitied. "Bless his heart" might have been used to describe him.

He went off to university and began to mature in academics and social interaction. He was embraced by his church with encouragement. He finished his junior year of college and went home before beginning his summer work.

He visited a minister's widow in his church. Her family was one of high achievers, demonstrated by her late husband, her three grown children, and her young grandchildren. She showed him their pictures and spoke of their achievements. They engaged in pleasant conversation and enjoyable refreshments. She handed him a folded newspaper.

He took the hometown newspaper and smiled. He thought she had read in the paper that he had been appointed as a summer missionary to an island in the Caribbean.

Then she said, "When I read this, I asked myself how could someone like you get to do something like this?"

He smiled and remained silent.

She repeated the question, waiting for an answer.

Reluctantly he said, "I guess because I applied." He never forgot her question, nor his response.

## Questions to Ponder

1. Was the older widow's comment helpful to the young man?
2. Who are the chosen?
3. How should the chosen be treated?

 

# Inasmuch

In any classroom or other social groups, often there is one child who is the victim of bullying. The child may be isolated, without a special friend, no one to sit with at lunch, and always the last one chosen as a team member. Being bullied can damage a childhood and subsequent adulthood. Issues of self-esteem, belief in self-efficacy, skill in social relationships, and experience in conflict resolutions may be impaired.

While it may become more sophisticated, bullying can continue into adulthood. In the church, the ministerial staff are prone to be bullied by frustrated and angry church members. These bullies may even be among the elected and ordained members of the church. Often restrained by their roles, ministers may not be able to respond to bullying as others might. The unspoken expectation may be that they must turn the other cheek and forgive. Their arsenal of response to bullying may be limited.

Congregations can be particularly cruel and dishonest. One moment ministers are held in high regard; the next moment they are church enemy number one. Words to the face and words behind the back are not always the same. One moment they are regarded as called of God, the next moment as working for us. Too many of us have witnessed unthinkable behavior toward staff. Too many have not attempted to thwart the bullying. Fear of being bullied inhibits responses at bullying prevention.

Non-constructive and ill-conceived ministerial criticism goes unchallenged. After all, ministerial staff are to follow the golden rule, even when being victimized by those with gilded rods. Behavior deemed unacceptable in other social contexts is accepted in church interactions. Some ministers may withdraw from paid ministry; some may continue to function, demoralized by the abuse, broken and disillusioned by God's redeemed.

Those onlookers who are silent about such abuse must assume culpability. The most powerful word to state, to reflect, and to call to action in such situations is Jesus' word "Inasmuch" (see Matthew 25).

## Questions to Ponder

1. Can you recall a ministerial staff member being bullied by church members? If so, explain.
2. How should the church respond to other members who are being bullied?
3. Recall Jesus' life recorded in Scripture. Was he bullied? Explain your response.

# Holy Parent of All Life

Holy Parent of all Life, past, present, and future, we come today in these few moments to give thanks for [add names] who serve our church and your church. We are grateful for the calling and specific direction given to each of them and to us their community. For some this specific call may have occurred early in life or in the middle of life, and for others it may be in the later stages of life. They reflect diversity of gifts, temperaments, and experiences. Each of these differences is a part of your holy creation and our human responses to your call. All of them make unique contributions to the work of your Kingdom. Thank you for their time of preparation, growth, and experience that makes their service with us more bountiful.

We ask that you help us to interact with them properly, respectfully, and supportively, always remembering that inasmuch as we have done unto the least of these, we have done unto you. Give each of them a shared vision for the future in which we all work together for things that are good. Guard and protect their physical and emotional health; meet their financial and social needs. Deepen their spiritual lives so we in turn may be deepened by their example. May [add names] be renewed with your abundant grace so they may witness to the One we all seek to serve. Forgive us when we have come short in supporting them; for in truth, we fall short in supporting you.

Thank you for Jesus the Christ who came to show us the Way. In the name of Jesus the Crucified, we pray. Amen.

 

# TIMES OF PATRIOTISM

*For our conversation is in heaven; from whence also we look for the Saviour,*
*the Lord Jesus Christ.*
—Philippians 3:20

*A man can be a Christian or a patriot, but he can't legally be a Christian and*
*a patriot—except in the usual way: one of the two with the mouth,*
*the other with the heart.*
—Mark Twain

*Fanaticism is governed by imagination rather than judgment.*
—Harriet Beecher Stowe

Flags of the United States are flying high on public buildings, in private businesses, in local churches, in homes, in public conversations, and on the backs of trucks. Patriotism has become publicly and politically popular. The national anthem, the Pledge of Allegiance, and photo sessions emphasize our loyalty to the nation—but not all so enthusiastically; others are on bended knees when national anthems and allegiances are proclaimed. Questions on patriotism are raised.

Displays of patriotism and celebration pose special considerations for the local church and among reflective Christians, much like the questions raised to Jesus and his classic answer of "render unto Caesar" (Matthew 22:21). Determining what to render unto Caesar is a perennial question that must be answered by individuals and by individual faith communities.

Today is a provocative time for both Christian and non-Christian populations on the question of patriotism and nationalism. How do we express appropriate appreciation for the land of our birth or our adoption and our ultimate loyalty to the Kingdom of God? We must exercise caution that we do not unquestionably equate the two as one. Issues such as the Pledge of Allegiance being said in the church sanctuary and the American flag displayed in the church sanctuary or on church property should be examined.

The Christian allegiance should be to widening circles of outreach of the Gospel, not to reducing the size of the circle to include only our own in terms of language, ethnicity, and other social characteristics. This section will not answer the important questions around patriotism, but it will provide resources that may inspire thought and discussion. Opening both our minds and our hearts should be the result of our being open to the Jesus of the Gospels.

The following pages provide supplemental resources that might enhance the preparation for celebrating patriotism. You will find several hymns, readings, stories and theological reflections, and a seasonal prayer. May these resources become a seasoning to add new flavor to this important observation. May this experience provide new imaginations, insights, and actions.

    

# We Thank Thee O Lord for Our Part in This Land

**Claude Douglas Bryan**

Suggested Tunes: I LOVE THEE
ST. DENIO
GORDON
Meter: 11.11.11.11.

We thank thee O Lord for our part in this land;
The dreams of our fathers and mothers we share;
With tears and with joy they take up their stand,
Upheld by thy grace in each struggle and care.

Our Father, we honor ones serving our land;
From farms and the cities they heard their land's call,
Defending, protecting by rightful command,
Bestowing their service in life for us all.

To islands and cities away they were sent;
They journeyed by air by the day and by night.
They paid the full cost for each time as they went;
In living and dying for all was their plight.

Now freedom this day is not ours alone;
Each legacy lives and shall always remain.
These heroes gave service and life for our own
Because of their toil may Ole Glory still reign.

Protect the protectors who daily still serve,
Defending our liberty's wonder for all.
Our God grant us wisdom in helping preserve
All freedom in work and in worship's true call.

Remind us O Lord freedom comes by thy grace;
Indebted are we for great Calvary's tree;
Our Christ both did live and did die for each race;
Together as one may we bow at his Knee.

# Widen Borders of Our Heart

**Claude Douglas Bryan**                    **Suggested Tunes: BEACH SPRINGS**
**HYMN TO JOY**
**Meter: 8.7.8.7.D.**

Daily citizens of two lands;
Kingdoms make their loyal claims.
Strife and tensions we each must live—
Earthly life and heavenly life.
Kingdom follows one way narrow,
Giving God first place in life;
Honor Jesus' love through justice;
Jesus' life and words must match.

Hearts and minds will shape behaviors;
Widen borders of our heart;
Understanding minds must grow;
Keep the Spirit's making new.
We give thanks for lands where we live;
Christ revealed in how we live;
Praising God for earth and heaven;
Living rightly here and then.

# Citizenship (Reading)

Heavenly Creator, we thank you for a place to live our lives where there is freedom for life, dreams, and hope. Thank you that we have continued to understand that these opportunities should exist for all people regardless of ethnicity. Thank you for those in our society who have advocated and who still advocate for freedom, dignity, and opportunity for all.

We thank you for the women and men who have given their service to protecting these opportunities for our nation and those whose service resulted in their death. We express our gratitude for each of those who have served us, not only in the military but also in government and in responsible citizenship.

May we be the salt and light in our citizenship by living the life of Jesus through the guidance and power of the Holy Spirit. May our citizenship in this place become an opportunity for us to share the freeing Gospel of Jesus Christ with all we encounter. We ask for guidance as we seek to discover and to live out our citizenship not only in this country but also within the greater Kingdom of God. Give us the wisdom to know the difference. May your Kingdom come on earth as it is in heaven. Help us be caring sisters and brothers to all. Amen.

# Two Flags Flying (Poem)

Two flags fly,
Each one calling,
Moving by wind,
Moving by mind.
One for physical rule,
One for spiritual rule,
One defines borders,
One knows no borders.

Two flags fly,
Each one speaking,
More than fabric,
More than colors.
Devotion called by each,
Loyalty called by each,
Sometimes in conflict,
Sometimes in harmony.

Two flags fly,
Each one raised,
Capturing devotion,
Demanding love.
Stitched by sacrifice,
Stitched by grace,
Rules not achieved,
Open to the future.

Two flags fly,
Each one lowered,
Asking deep questions,
Giving deep answers.
Stitched by love,
Raised in pride,
Commitment waving,
Commitment waiting.

## Questions to Ponder

1. What conflict is the author addressing for the Christian?
2. What does it mean to "render unto Caesar" and "render unto God"?
3. How do you personally respond to the issues raised by loyalty to nation and loyalty to God?

# Just Right

The middle school class was studying a basic overview of the concepts of civics. They focused on learning terms, concepts, and the differences among them.

"What is the difference between patriotism and nationalism?" one student asked his teacher.

"Let's have an object lesson to begin to talk about the differences between nationalism and patriotism," the teacher said. "Gather around the sink."

She placed a potted plant in the sink.

"Is water good?" she asked.

Loud "yeses" were shouted.

"Is water needed for life?" the teacher asked.

Loud "yeses" were shouted once more.

"What happens if we have too little water?"

"Doesn't do any good," one student offered.

"Okay, what else?" asked the teacher. The teacher held up the plant.

"If you're a plant and you don't get enough water, you die," one student said.

"What about too much water?" the teacher asked.

"Too much can also kill plants."

"It washes away the soil."

"The roots can rot."

"Good responses," the teacher said, "That might be an effective way to begin our discussion on patriotism and nationalism."

"So," one student said, "too much can kill you and not enough can do you no good."

"Well done. Back to your seats," the teacher said.

## Questions to Ponder

1. How do you differentiate between patriotism and nationalism?

2. Should Christians be patriotic? Explain.

3. What happens if Christianity and nationalism are considered one and the same?

## Flags and Faith

"If you don't like it, leave it." These words were sung by a Western movie and TV couple in the early 1970s on a popular Sunday night variety show. Not being part of a churchgoing family, I was able to watch the show on our new color television set. This song of patriotism was sung in response to growing student unrest and the Vietnam conflict. It was easy to be part of the patriotic sentiment. I thought little about it.

Years later I would go on one of my favorite activities—a trip to the thrift store. This trip included my mother-in-law. Inside a glass case, I saw a small kitchen strainer with its handle painted red, white, and blue.

I asked my mother-in-law, "How old do you think the strainer is?"

She said, "I would imagine from the 1940s and 1950s."

"Interesting the choice of colors," I said.

"Yes, we were very patriotic," she responded.

I remember making the metaphoric statement to my college class: "It is difficult to analyze the air we breathe when that very air has influenced the oxygenation of our bloodstream and consequently nurtured our brains." Class discussion ensued. I elaborated on how challenging it is to question ideas that have been a part of our socialization, especially our religion. Our ethnocentrism makes it difficult to be objective about ourselves and our social groups. I went on to describe how patriotism and Christianity have long been intertwined. Objective analysis is often hindered by emotion.

These three incidents have emerged in greater clarity and focus. I have watched worship services and political rhetoric on social media. Christian nationalism, of which I have grown increasingly fearful, is swelling in the United States. I saw a woman minister, whom I applauded, speaking, and close to her and on camera was an American flag. I was uncomfortable. I love the flag of my country; however, I have a greater love for following God. I was uneasy about the possible double and confusing message. I have always been distressed by films depicting the rise of German Nazism with the background music of familiar hymns.

The struggles for living when we have both a Christian citizenship and a national citizenship are multiple. Which one has the greater influence on the other? Mrs. John Benson's hymn "This World Is Not My Home" (see https://hymnary.org/text/ive_left_the_land_of_death_and_sin) reminds us that his world is our current, though not ultimate, home. Which flag shall we salute and pledge?

## Questions to Ponder

1. Can you think of ways we link national pride and Christianity? Explain.
2. Do you believe it is difficult to be objective about patriotism? Explain.
3. Do you believe it is difficult to be objective about Christianity? Explain.
4. Is objectivity important to any such discussion? Explain.

# God of All Nations

God of all nations, we acknowledge that we have dual citizenship, one in the Kingdom of God and one in our earthly nation. Scripture records Jesus' teaching that we must render unto Caesar the things that belong to Caesar and unto God the things that belong to God. May we ponder this mysterious statement, pausing to consider what God owns and what the nation owns regarding our loyalty. The ancient Hebrews cried unto God for a king, like the kings of the non-Hebrews around them. Scripture records God's reluctant willingness to honor the request. A classic dilemma is recorded for readers today—loyalty to God and loyalty to the state. Their subsequent history records more times of religious-political division than times of religious-political harmony.

Help us grasp that our flag is not the only flag that reigns in the world. Theologically, each temporal flag is displayed on the same level in the parade of flags. Each nation, even those with acknowledged political issues and conflicts, is loved by her citizenship, even by her Christian citizens. There are many national anthems that move citizens to emotional allegiance and pride. Ours is not the only country with purple mountains, blue skies, and amber waves of grain.

Provide spiritual light and insight as we discern what it means to render unto Caesar and render unto God. Keep us focused as we worship you and give appropriate honor and allegiance above all other loyalties. May we participate with you in creating a genuine brotherhood and sisterhood extending beyond geographical divisions. Let us demonstrate Christ-like love toward all who live within our nation with various languages, customs, and faiths; and let us demonstrate Christ-like love to those who live in other nations with various languages, customs, and faiths. May we learn to worship you and love others. In the name of Jesus the Crucified, we pray. Amen.

# TIMES OF PEACE

*Depart from evil, and do good; seek peace, and pursue it.*
—Psalm 34:14

*Peace is more important than all justice; and peace was not made for the sake of justice, but justice for the sake of peace.*
—Martin Luther

*The world would have peace if only men of politics would follow the Gospel.*
—St. Bridget of Sweden

*When two elephants fight it is the grass that gets hurt.*
—African Proverb

Close your eyes and imagine that you're living in a foreign capital as a trusted guard to a high-ranking official. In fact, you're doing alright. Your life is peaceful. Your brother, having returned from the homeplace, stops to visit. You ask the customary question, "How are the old friends doing and how's the old neighborhood?" You expect to receive the comforting response of "things are okay" or "not much has changed." Instead, suddenly, you're introduced to the disturbing reality. Things aren't well in the neighborhood. Those at home are in trouble and disgrace. The city gates have been burned. Attacks are a real threat.

The biblical character Nehemiah had such an experience. Responding to the bad news, Nehemiah cried, gave up eating, and prayed. He engaged in theological reflections on Hebrew Scripture, God's promises, human actions, and world conditions. Both the guilty and the innocent were caught up in the consequences of unfaithfulness to God. Nehemiah acknowledged the disobedience and recalled the promises of God. If the unfaithful would turn faithful, there would be restoration. Nehemiah asked that God hear not only his prayer but also the prayers of other servants. After reflection, he asked for God's favor in how he must respond. Using his resources as a cupbearer, Nehemiah approached King Artaxerxes, who inquired about Nehemiah's troubled state. Nehemiah explained and requested to return to rebuild his homeland. The king agreed and Nehemiah participated in God's restoration of his people.

Nehemiah knew that to have real peace, real peace must exist for all people and not for him alone. Should we do less? The church has a unique calling to promote a holistic and healthy peace within the individual and among individuals. Do we pray for peace for ourselves and for others? Like Nehemiah, are we willing to meet human need and to alleviate suffering and to assist in bringing peace and wholeness to all?

The following pages provide supplemental resources that might enhance the preparation for the celebration of and promotion of peace. You will find several hymns, readings, stories and theological reflections, and a seasonal prayer. May these resources become a seasoning to add new flavor to this important celebration. May you experience new imaginations, insights, and actions.

 

# Bring Eternal Peace We Pray

**Claude Douglas Bryan**

**Suggested Tunes: DIX
REDHEAD**
**Meter:** 7.7.7.7.7.7.

Bless the ones who serve their land
Through her times of war and peace;
Guard their moments where they stand;
Grant that times of war may cease.
Now forgive us lest we stray—
Bring eternal peace we pray.

Those who answer country's call,
Sons and daughters loved since birth,
Safely keep all lest they fall;
Create peace and joy on earth.
Now forgive us lest we stray—
Bring eternal peace we pray.

Fathers, mothers serve their lands;
Comfort those still left behind;
Rescue all with healing hands;
Wounds be healed and lives refined.
Now forgive us lest we stray—
Bring eternal peace we pray.

Bless those on the other side;
All are made from sacred art.
May we all be unified—
Brothers, sisters with one heart.
Now forgive us lest we stray—
Bring eternal peace we pray.

# Precious Savior, Peace Incarnate

**Claude Douglas Bryan**　　　　Suggested Tunes: HYMN TO JOY
AUSTRIAN HYMN
ELLESDIE
**Meter: 8.7.8.7.D.**

Precious Savior, Peace Incarnate,
Son of Man who came to save;
Heaven's watch care, God's own mandate;
May our wait for thee not waive.

Dismal darkness, desolation;
Healings, cleansings for our ill;
Come now, fill us, Consolation;
May our hearts in thee be still.

Gracious Giver, Healing Herald,
All in need find strength through thee;
Blest Redeemer, Champion's Call-ed,
Give us courage to be free.

May we walk this day in calmness,
Touched by faith, a wondrous gift.
Through our sadness and in gladness,
Mercy's wings bestow thy lift.

Take our scars and sorrows stinging;
Purge our pain now into praise;
Grant redemption in our living;
We proclaim thee all our days.

Let us share this message boldly—
God in Christ has overcome.
Foe and woe all, Christ shall make flee;
Victors, too, we can become.

# Prince of Peace (Poem)

Prince of Peace, who loves all kinds,
Save us even though we fall.
Shape our actions, hearts, and minds
Into love for one and all.
Now forgive us lest we stray–
Bring eternal peace we pray.

## Questions to Ponder

1. What does it mean to be "Prince of Peace"?
2. What is a biblical understanding of peace? Explain.
3. Are there implications if we identify Jesus as "Prince of Peace"? Explain.

# Peace (Monologue)

I am Peace. Some people have misunderstandings in exactly who I am. Sometimes I am described in the negative, in what I am not and not in what I am. Some think I exist when the war stops. When the fighting ceases, I am created. But premature peace or undeveloped peace may encourage the birth of future wars and conflict. Once the peace settlements have settled with demands and consequences, often they become the seedbeds of anger and future conflict.

No, that's not who I am or where I exist. Some people believe I exist in silence. Those who cannot hear noises may assume there is peace. Whether there is silence or noise, there may be voices that have yet to be heard or needs that have yet to be expressed. Anger may be born in silence and erupt in violence.

Where there is an all-or-none competition or mentality, I often cannot live. Where there is unwarranted or unproductive criticism, I often cannot live. Where there are harsh words, I often cannot live. Where there is a world of haves and have-nots, I cannot live. All of these are not conducive to bringing me forth.

I may best be understood in biblical wholeness. I dwell best in the lives of women and men, brothers and sisters, who have genuine mutual concern for the benefit of the other. Simply put, peace exists where the whole needs of the whole are met. Peace exists where there is concern for alleviating poverty, injustice, discrimination, ill will, preferential treatment, or arguments. I exist where people are not afraid. Being afraid produces anything but peace, not only in the individual but also in surrounding lives. When people are afraid, they act out. Acting out encourages others to act out. I, Peace, cannot exist.

How can I, Peace, flourish? Developing empathy for one another encourages the birth of me. Making sure there is equity in the distribution of basic resources and opportunities assists me to grow. I exist where there is a mutual submission among all. Peace exists when people put the needs of others first, creating a mutual community of concern.

Peace is anything but cheap. I come with a heavy price. Peace involves submitting self-interest and trusting that others will do likewise. Only peace within can produce peace without. Most importantly, people alone cannot achieve me, but I am achieved by their participation with God's grace. God offers peace as wholeness, shalom for all. Peace exists through the self-sacrificing love found in Jesus the Christ. If you would know me, you must know him. You must seek him with all your heart. Blessed are the peacemakers, for they shall know God.

# Peace Through Empathy

Peace is often defined as a lack of conflict or the cessation of war. The war had raged on for years. Names of the enemy's leaders had been posted in print and on social media. One day the announcement was made that a leader of a terrorist group had been caught and killed. Words of praise were given upon this death of one who had caused the deaths of so many.

Even in the church, people were glad. One woman who had lost her son in the war was quiet. An adolescent asked, "Why are you so quiet? Are you not happy the terrorist has been killed?"

"It's not that easy," she said. "I am glad that there will be no more deaths caused by his actions. However, his death is not to be praised."

"Why not?" the patriotic father of the adolescent asked.

"His death, too, must be mourned. It reflects the failure of the human heart, his own and perhaps even our own."

"I don't understand," the father said.

"Did we contribute to the anger, hatred, and aggression that he showed?" another asked.

The woman paused, waiting for someone else to speak. No one did.

Finally, she broke the silence. "I lost my only son in this war," she said. "The terrorist just killed is the son of a mother and a father, too. I mourn for them as well. I mourn for him and what his life might've been."

## Questions to Ponder

1. Is peace cheap or costly?
2. Does peace involve forgiveness?
3. Does peace promote peace?
4. What role does empathy play in promoting peace and justice?

 

# Peace Under the Rug

"We have been able to stay together by avoiding anything controversial," she explained to me one day.

We were discussing how a church like ours could flourish given the wide diversity within our congregation.

"How have you done that?" I asked.

"We don't talk about it in public. We avoid things controversial such as politics," she added.

"When there is genuine and worthy conflict, what do you do?" I asked.

"It is sad to say, we sweep it under the rug," she said.

"I suppose that has kept rug makers in business," I commented.

I understood what she meant. Peace at all costs.

We discovered that eventually the church carpet became hazardous because of the unspoken conflict it covered. It was hard to walk without stumbling because of this hidden dirt. Hidden dirt has a mind of its own. It grows more powerful and invasive with the passing years. What is not spoken grows powerfully, waiting for the time to rear its angry hydra head.

After various German invasions, noted British political leader Neville Chamberlain sought to reassure anxious Europeans that there would be peace. The pronouncement did not last long with the onset of World War II.

We stopped sweeping when the rugs imploded.

## Questions to Ponder

1. Is there a time to sweep conflict under the rug? Explain.
2. Do you agree that unexpressed conflicts grow? Explain.
3. How can genuine peace be promoted? Explain.

# God of Peace

God of Peace who proclaimed the creation good, we acknowledge that we have led lives that have not promoted peace for all. We have exploited lands, resources, people, and opportunities that were not ours. Instead, we have promoted peace and prosperity for ourselves alone. Help us this day to understand that we cannot have individual peace if others do not have the same peace. Scripture proclaims that God is the Prince of Peace. Those who follow the Prince of Peace must live in peace with each other—not a peace that is the absence of noise and voices but a peace that listens to the cries of those in need and those who express anger for inequities. Take us to a place where we might all live in harmony with each other. Transform our local political parties into universal peace parties. Transform us.

Show us the specific ways to promote peace, and give us the energy and devotion to practice those behaviors. Let us provide for those who need childcare, let us provide affordable education, let us provide economic opportunity, let us promote honest conversation, and let us promote acceptance when there is a difference of opinions. Peace is wholeness for all of God's creation. May our petitions for peace and wellness include petitions for peace and wellness for all. Let us work toward the peace that passes all understanding. Let us each ask, What can I do to promote peace for my brothers and sisters? In the name of Jesus the Crucified, we pray. Amen.

# TIMES OF PENTECOST AND MISSIONS

*And when the day of Pentecost was fully come,*
*they were all with one accord in one place.*
—Acts 2:1


*The Christian shoemaker does his duty not by putting little crosses on the shoes,*
*but by making good shoes, because God is interested in good craftsmanship.*
—Martin Luther


*I shall go wherever I am asked to participate for freedom.*
—Mary Tyler Peabody Mann

Observed approximately fifty days after Easter, Pentecost has come. We are filled with the Spirit. What are we to do next? Jesus said that he would return. What do we do in the meantime? How do we live from Pentecost forward? After all, it has been almost two thousand years since the Pentecost event. One answer is "living between the times" and carrying out our mission of sharing God's love in its fullest dimension.

Following Pentecost came the command and the ability to go forward in living and proclaiming the Gospel. We are called to be new brothers and sisters to one another, not having the rivalry that so often accompanies siblings who compete for the attention of parents. God in his infinite mercy has offered attention, acceptance, and renewal to each of us; and in turn, we are to share in living out his love with the communities in which we are called. Is there consistency and integrity with who you are and how you live? How do you live with your family, your church, your work, and your community? Provide encouragement to those with hurts, joys, losses, victories, and even doubts—to those struggling around you. We should share our lives between the times.

When we must live with unanswered questions, when we must work with hostile people, when we must give a word of encouragement even though we ourselves are so fragile, when we must experience personal and professional rejection, and when we must confront hostile criticism, our human tendency is to stop. Little voices may creep into our minds with their haunting questions. Why bother? What's the use? Does anyone care?

Continue to be involved in being a good communicator of the Gospel when opportunity occurs. Let your communities grow. Live in community with one another and not in competition with each other. Live in ultimate loyalty and not in compromise to the One who called you. Work hard and do not grow weary, so that you might be a faithful witness to the Gospel. Let this filling of the Spirit, this Pentecost, move you to communicate your service.

The following pages provide supplemental resources that might enhance the preparation for the celebration of Pentecost and missions. You will find several hymns, readings, stories and theological reflections, and a seasonal prayer. May these resources become a seasoning to add new flavor to this important celebration. May you experience new imaginations, insights, and actions.

 

# Will You Go If Christ Calls You?

**Claude Douglas Bryan**

**Suggested Tune: HENDON**
**Meter: 7 .7.7.7.7.**

Will you go if Christ calls you?
Answers to his call are due;
Lives set free but free to serve
Him in all that he deserves.
Will you go if Christ calls you?

Many called but chosen few
'Cept those hearing all to do;
Boundless measures of thy grace
Given to the human race.
Will you go if Christ calls you?

Life alone is not our call;
God's redemption is for all;
Those with voices still must speak
For the hopeless and the weak.
Will you go if Christ calls you?

We must move beyond our reach;
Hearts to love and minds to teach.
Christ incarnate in our world,
Showing God's great plan for all.
Will you go if Christ calls you?

Help me, Lord, to be the one
Serving thee till all is done;
Not with comfort safe indeed
With thy people still in need.
Will you go if Christ calls you?

Life becomes a holy quest
For those loving him the best;
Called to go or called to stay,
Yielded still in every way.
Will you go if Christ calls you?

# Whispers from the Savior

**Claude Douglas Bryan**

**Suggested Tune: WYE VALLEY**
**Meter: 6.5.6.5.D. with Refrain**

Whispers from the Savior
Give us breath this day.
Peace creates behavior;
Grace now guides the way.
Love outpoured on Cal'vry
Shall not be in vain.
Mercy must not tarry;
Free we shall remain.
Whispers from the Savior
Our hearts long to hear.
We need holy presence—
Christ to us draw near.

Let us share the mission
With our Lord today.
Show us thy petition
In all we should say.
May we share the story
With each one in need,
God's redemption's glory—
Love in word and deed.
Whispers from the Savior
Our hearts long to hear.
We need holy presence—
Christ to us draw near.

Show us our true calling—
Many parts we play.
Clear our ears for hearing,
Only Christ obey.
Guide us now to our place
Where we are thy tool.
May we run the good race—
Live the golden rule.
Whispers from the Savior
Our hearts long to hear.
We need holy presence—
Christ to us draw near.

## We Are Called To Serve (Responsive Reading)

LEADER: God, the Creator of all creation, invites us to live as new citizens within the Kingdom of God where all human life—each gender, each age, and each ethnicity—is sacred.

PEOPLE: Praise be to God for this great invitation.

LEADER: God, who became flesh through Jesus the Christ, invites us to serve one another in both the giving of ministry and the receiving of ministry.

PEOPLE: Praise be to God for this great invitation.

LEADER: God, the Sustainer of all life, invites us to live in peace and wholeness as church and family, as brothers and sisters.

PEOPLE: Praise be to God for this great invitation.

LEADER: God, the Great I Am, invites us to use our given gifts and our opportunities in the Kingdom of God where the greatest gift and opportunity is the exercise of love.

PEOPLE: Praise be to God for this great invitation.

LEADER: God invites us not to govern one another but to serve one another with wisdom and with love in both the seen and the unseen.

PEOPLE: Praise be to God for this great invitation.

*ALL:* Let us respond yes to this great invitation by serving as we are gifted, by serving as we are given opportunity, and by serving as we are loved by God. Praise be to God.

# Pentecost (Poem)

A number gathered there to wait and watch,
Praying, praising, and pausing,
Not moving until God first moved.
Like fires from heaven came the replay,
Filling each with the power and love of God,
New languages they could now speak.
Each one understood the Gospel in his or her own language,
Venturing out to share the story in ways understood.

Now we are called to be the communicators
Who carry the message to every land and people.
Not a message born and sustained by humankind,
A message born and lived by God on earth.
This message of God's power to accept and to renew,
Breathing into the creation a new gift of life.
Breath that empowers what we were intended to be,
Telling the fullness of God's message of redemption.

## Questions to Ponder

1. What do you believe is the significance of Pentecost?
2. Does Pentecost have a message for readers and hearers today? Explain.

 

# Might Be You

The calendar reminded the church that it was time to emphasize the offering for missions. All the classes were invited to participate, from the youngest to the oldest. The teacher had just talked with her children's class about Pentecost. She announced the class's participation in the offering. She asked if there were any questions.

"Why do we have to go and help those people?" the class asked. "Why should we work and collect money to bring gifts to them? Why can't they get it for themselves?"

The wise teacher said, "Remember, when you're called upon to do something that's hard for someone, you might one day be that person. You might be the person who has no parents and who lives with a single grandmother. You might be the child who doesn't have food, except for the food given to her at school. You might be the child that's picked on and harassed during the day. Always remember, it might be you."

"And it is Jesus," one thoughtful child said.

"Yes, Pentecost in action," the teacher said.

## Questions to Ponder

1. Was the child's response about Jesus appropriate? Explain.
2. What did the teacher mean by the words "Pentecost in action"? Explain.
3. Can remembering Jesus make a difference in how we respond to people and to opportunities? Explain.

## Waiting and Ascending

The flight was at night from a small regional airport. I went through the ticketing process and sat down in the departing area, waiting for the call for departure. One airline attendant stood at the counter, and I alone sat in the waiting area. Time passed with no announcement of boarding. My concern heightened. It was my first flight. I approached the counter and inquired about the flight. The attendant looked up, and his facial expressions indicated that he had forgotten about me. He helped with my bag and quickly led me to the tarmac. The door to the plane was closed. What do I do? I knocked on the door and asked sheepishly, "May I come in?" The door opened and I boarded the plane. Eventually we ascended into the night sky—a unique time and place.

Christian formation or Christian development occurs through various interactions such as reading, listening, observing, and most importantly participating. Building on foundations established by other interactions, participation allows for deeper and more permanent change. As the famous American educator John Dewey would emphasize, we learn by doing.

On the Christian calendar is a day called Pentecost, fifty days after Ascension Day. Before Pentecost were days when followers waited before venturing forward. I suspect those days were filled with wonder, conversation, prayer, anticipation, impatience, doubts, and fears. With Pentecost, these early followers received the empowering of the Holy Spirit that enabled new life and mission. We do not know the mechanics of how this mystery happened, only that it happened.

My first flight was to a weekend orientation for students to spend the summer overseas as what we termed a summer missionary. For a Baptist student, this opportunity was a big deal. I stayed at what was nicknamed the Lottie Moon Hilton, a residential complex at the Baptist Foreign Mission Board in Richmond, Virginia. I remember the excitement of the Saturday evening worship service led by a famous and revered Baptist missionary head, Dr. James Cauthen. His remarks were serious, sobering, challenging, and invitational. He spoke of passports, inoculations, correspondence, gathering materials, and packing—all of these at the same time of completing an academic semester. There were only forty days to wait, which seemed a lifetime to me. So much to do and so little time to do it.

 

In numerous ways, my Christian discipleship has been the product of involvement in mission endeavors in both the United States and beyond. Most of these experiences have been international, but several were in unfamiliar parts of the United States. Opportunities came that I might provide service in such places as New York, Colorado, the Cayman Islands, Nigeria, Hong Kong, Lithuania, Romania, and the Philippines. These were diverse geographic regions, languages, and cultures. What did I learn from these experiences? I learned confidence to take chances and risks; to put myself center stage when needed and to be content in backstage roles; to recognize each diversity of people who loved their own land and heritage; and to link the content of messages and the actions of behaviors in consistent ways. Sometimes I perceived success and other times not so much success.

I had been inspired by the words attributed to William Carey, the father of the modern missionary movement: "Expect great things for God, attempt great things for God." Soon I learned that mission endeavors, especially the popular short-term ones, make at least an equal impact on the missionary as on the actual mission. What people learn by involvement with diverse others opens new learning about themselves, their beliefs, and their commitments.

In my younger years, my goal was to do important things for God; in my older years, I followed one of Hippocrates' admonitions—do no harm. The novel *The Ugly American* depicts an attitude and impression that Americans have often created. Bad behavior, especially when done in the name of religion, is noticed and remembered. An innocent or habitual word may discredit Christian messages. Keep the words simple and the actions well-informed. Wait and ascend.

## Questions to Ponder

1. Do you believe that Pentecost and missions are related? Explain.

2. If you have had mission experiences, what personal changes, if any, occurred? Were these permanent or temporary?

3. What does the author mean by doing no harm regarding missions?

4. What value do missionary endeavors and commitments have for the local church?

# God of Pentecost and Missions

God of Pentecost and missions, fill us with both your spirit and your direction. In our goings and comings, show us opportunities both near and far to share in various ways the Good News of God's compassion for all humanity. While we may not speak the unfamiliar languages of others, may we learn to communicate the language of self-sacrificial love. Empowered by the Spirit, may we learn to convey the basic Gospel message that transcends cultural differences. May our own ingrained and appreciated culture not impede a clear and honest communication of the Gospel. Forgive any barriers that we or our forefathers and foremothers have created that hinder this sacred message and our participation. Let our minds know the differences between Gospel messages and cultural preferences. In our missions, may we seek to show only the way of Jesus.

Show us patience as we share the daily lives of those who may not know the love of God. Forgive us as we fail. May we treat others as equals, speaking in the power of God's love to brothers and sisters yet unknown. While we may always speak with earthly regional accents, may we speak plainly the message created for all creation. Let us be where there is need for water, for education, for food, for housing, for friendship, for justice, and for you. Let us not ask "if we should go" but "why should we not go." In the name of Jesus the Crucified, we pray. Amen.

# TIMES OF TEACHING AND LEARNING

*Let the word of Christ dwell in you richly in all wisdom; teaching and admonishing one another in psalms and hymns and spiritual songs, singing with grace in your hearts to the Lord.*
—Colossians 3:16

*A teacher who is attempting to teach without inspiring the pupil with a desire to learn is hammering on cold iron.*
—Horace Mann

*Knowledge is a garden. If it isn't cultivated, you can't harvest it.*
—African Proverb

Teaching and learning are essential elements of congregational life. In any part of the church building, teaching and learning are occurring: in committee meetings, in the preschool area, or in the worship service. We need teachers and learners. While teaching and learning are essential to all age groups for growth, teaching is critical to the next generation.

Teaching and learning are vital to impact the next generations of our congregation. Consider Hannah and her son Samuel. Samuel was brought for training in serving God. Each year Hannah would visit her son, who was entrusted to Eli's care. Each yearly visit involved bringing a new robe for Samuel to account for his growth during the previous year. Old robes were good only for a limited season. (See 1 Samuel 2.)

Like Hannah, we are called to make robes for a new generation. We are to dedicate that generation to God and to lead by the best example, knowing that the next generation is ultimately not ours but God's. Robes, as a metaphor, must be the provisions that allow the learners to grow, neither too large nor too small. We must provide for their needs and growth. We must teach not only the next generation but also the current generation. Teaching and learning are central in our Gospel transmission. No one is too young or too old.

The following pages provide supplemental resources that might enhance the preparation for observing and emphasizing teaching and learning. You will find several hymns, readings, stories and theological reflections, and a seasonal prayer. May these resources become a seasoning to add new flavor to this important emphasis. May you experience new imaginations, insights, and actions.

 

# Thank You, Lord, for Ones Who Guided

**Claude Douglas Bryan**                    **Suggested Tunes: BEACH SPRING**
                                                                    **HYFRYDOL**
                                                                    **CASSELL**
                                                    **Meter: 8.7.8.7. D.**

Thank you, Lord, for ones who guided, seeing vision faith could see;
Loving patience they provided; help us find what we're to be.
Thank you, Lord, for gentle teachers, shaping hearts and minds to grow;
Showing care for heaven's creatures; share this love we've come to know.

Thank you, Lord, for ones of courage, who gave hopes for journeys long.
Freedom gained from final bondage; kept us safe from pathways wrong.
Thank you, Lord, for ones of vision, who saw dawnings through the
    night,
Keeping faith in life's decisions; led us forward through God's light.

Thank you, Lord for ones departed—earthly time and life now done;
Leaving us with peace imparted, till life's true completion won.
Thank you, Lord, for saving power—fashion sinners into saints.
Keeping life and faith in each hour, may Christ's love have no restraints.

 

# Lesson of the Day

**Claude Douglas Bryan**

**Suggested Tunes: DIX
RATISBON**
**Meter: 7.7.7.7.7.7.**

For the lesson of the day, for the challenge of this hour;
For the God who cares to teach, told again to help us learn;
Thankful for the Words of God, teaching all that we must learn.

For the message of your love, in our sin and disbelief;
By the blood of him who died, to reveal the way of love;
Thankful for the Words of God, teaching all that we must learn.

In the daily turns of life, there to guide us once again;
To paths of righteousness we walk, in step keep we with our God;
Thankful for the Words of God, teaching all that we must learn.

For the trials we must face, in the stresses we must bear;
All become a greater good, fashioned to the Son of Man;
Thankful for the Words of God, teaching all that we must learn.

Let us love each place you lead, where we may become like thee;
God's great power shall overcome, every hurt and each offense;
Thankful for the Words of God, teaching all that we must learn.

Life becomes one lesson long, blest by providence of God;
Not a moment is misused, but each used for his design;
Thankful for the Words of God, teaching all that we must learn.

 

# Help Us, O Lord, in Our Sacred Call

**Claude Douglas Bryan**

**Suggested Tune: REDEEMER**
**Meter: 9 .9.9.9. with Refrain**

Help us, O Lord, in our sacred call;
Teach we thy Word and works now to all;
Students whose needs become our first charge,
Hearts and minds we too would enlarge.
Lord of Creation, Shepherd of shepherds,
Bless now vocations and plans yet to be.
Anxious and willing to do thy bidding,
Teaching and guiding students for thee.

Knowing and being blend into thee;
Truth yet discovered shall bow its knee;
Art and all science, they are thine own.
To Christ in whom truth may be made known.
Lord of Creation, Shepherd of Shepherds,
Bless now vocations and plans yet to be.
Anxious and willing to do thy bidding,
Teaching and guiding students for thee.

Now we unite who teach in this place,
Seeking the best in thy love and grace.
Sharing our knowledge gained in thy name;
Giving as given, God's truth proclaim.
Lord of Creation, Shepherd of Shepherds,
Bless now vocations and plans yet to be.
Anxious and willing to do thy bidding,
Teaching and guiding students for thee.

# The Gift of Thy Calling (Responsive Reading)

LEADER: Being a teacher is a high calling, a privilege, and a responsibility. Lord, we praise thee for giving us a place in thy world, a place to serve, a place to teach.

**PEOPLE:** We thank thee, Lord, for the gift of thy calling.

LEADER: Being a teacher demands a commitment of quantity and quality, time and energy, talent and life. Just as our Lord has committed himself to care for each of us, we commit ourselves to one another, to our students, and to our Lord.

**PEOPLE:** We thank thee, Lord, for the gift of thy calling.

LEADER: Being a teacher means being a craftsman, an artist. Help us, O God, to continue to grow in our art, in our profession, so we might be found pleasing to thee.

**PEOPLE:** We thank thee, Lord, for the gift of thy calling.

LEADER: Being a teacher means living in community with one another. Our Father, help us to remember that we are a part of a massive world but only a small part of a world created and sustained by thee.

**PEOPLE:** We thank thee, Lord, for the gift of thy calling.

LEADER: Being a teacher means challenging one another, our students, and ourselves. Teach us, O Creator, how to encourage one another in how we reason, in how we respond, and in how we love.

**PEOPLE:** We thank thee, Lord, for the gift of thy calling.

LEADER: Being a teacher means confronting truth and confronting evil. Our Father, strengthen us not to be content to remain within the safety of our current knowledge, the safety of our well-read books and notes, but strengthen us to move into thy world that needs the knowledge of the Savior.

**PEOPLE:** We thank thee, Lord, for the gift of thy calling.

 

LEADER: Being a teacher means having the willingness to continue in the calling, in our art. Empower us, our Lord, to preserve, to fight the good fight, and not to be content with less than we can be.

**PEOPLE:** We thank thee, Lord, for the gift of thy calling.

LEADER: For thy Son, Jesus, who died that we might have life, we praise thy Holy Name.

**PEOPLE:** We thank thee, Lord, for the gift of thy calling.

# Those Who Lead and Those Who Follow
## (Responsive Reading)

LEADER: Our Holy God, we come this morning acknowledging you as the Creator, the Redeemer, and the Sustainer of the world. You breathed life into being through your spoken Word. In your image and from the dust of the ground, we were created. Your spirit breathed life into our beings, allowing us to have the joy of fellowship with you and with one another as brother and sister. We live in a world that is fallen and broken, where both good and evil reside and where discernment is not always easy. In the midst of our struggles, we ask ourselves the ancient question:

**PEOPLE:** "Am I my brother and [sister's] keeper?" (Genesis 4:9)

LEADER: We were created to be one family, priests to all nations, one community keeping watch over the needs of one other. Forgive us where we have failed. We have worshiped you in ways that are self-serving and unloving. Often we do not follow the way of peace, the way of concern, the way of brother and sisterhood, the way of justice and peace. How can we challenge the evil around us? What do you require of us?

**PEOPLE:** "…To do justly, and to love mercy, and to walk humbly with thy God" (Micah 6:8).

LEADER: We are grateful for those who have the courage to lead and to guide us in these troubling times of violence, inequalities, unrest, exploitation, and change. For those who serve by protecting us through the military system, through the police system, through local, national, and world government, we remember God's Word:

**PEOPLE:** "Obey them that have the rule over you, and submit yourselves: for they watch for your souls, as they that must give account, that they may do it with joy, and not with grief: for that is unprofitable for you" (Hebrews 13:17).

LEADER: We pray for those who now serve and for those who are now departed through service. Their examples of courage and commitment live in our memories. For the living and the departed, bless their families, bless those with illness and disabilities, bless those with financial needs, and bless the grief that their absence has created in the lives of family, friends, and community. How shall we, as ambassadors of Christ, respond to those leaders and their families?

**PEOPLE:** "Rejoice with them that do rejoice, and weep with them that weep" (Romans 12:15).

LEADER: Holy One revealed in Jesus of Nazareth, you have taught us to render unto Caesar the things that are Caesar's and unto God the things that are God's. Give us wisdom to discern that which belongs to government and that which belongs to God. What is such wisdom?

**PEOPLE:** "…Behold, the fear of the LORD, that is wisdom; and to depart from evil is understanding" (Job 28:28).

LEADER: We pray that individuals would come forth to lead and to serve each and all of us as one people composed of many different languages, different vocabularies, different skin colors, different ethnic backgrounds, different thoughts and views, and even different faith expressions. Give leaders, both current and future, the ability to seek and to understand the Divine, to dispense justice and mercy equally among people, and to promote the interests of all and not only of those in power. What does Scripture declare that we are to do?

**PEOPLE:** "I exhort therefore, that, first of all, supplications, prayers, intercessions, and giving of thanks, be made for all men; For kings, and for all that are in authority; that we may lead a quiet and peaceable life in all godliness and honesty. For this is good and acceptable in the sight of God our Saviour" (1 Timothy 2:1-3).

LEADER: How shall we live in this way?

*ALL:* "Looking unto Jesus the author and finisher of our faith…" (Hebrews 12:2). Amen.

# "Yes, You Can"

The cohort class had finished its formal education courses with passing grades. Successful mastery of information, critical thinking and application, classroom management, and classroom lesson plans occurred. Supervised teaching was successful.

The cohort advisor gathered the soon-to-be graduates one last time. "I want to share with the class three of the most important words a teacher can say to a student. You must use these wisely. However, these words need to be heard by all students in some context." The advisor wrote on the whiteboard, in large letters, the following words: "Yes, You Can."

The advisor said, "Learners need the affirmation, the recognition, the opportunity, the reinforcement, the permission, the feedback, and the faith as we convey these words—'Yes, You Can.' Give it to them liberally but also with integrity."

## Questions to Ponder

1. What power has the word "yes" had in your life?
2. What happens when you say "no" to others?
3. Does saying "yes" and "no" have implications in Christian faith? Explain.

     

# I Said What?

I was working on my office computer developing a lesson plan. The phone rang and I answered by following my customary script—giving my name and my academic department and asking if I could assist. A voice no longer familiar identified himself as Joel. Joel had been a student years ago when I worked full-time in the classroom.

"I was just rearranging my office and saw your book on my shelf," he said.

"Really?" I responded, unsure of where this conversation was leading. Joel, though a congenial and gentle person, was one of my more conservative students who had chosen to go to a conservative theological seminary to find a suitable church position at a genuine Bible-believing and practicing church, whatever that meant.

He and another fellow student had visited me once following their graduation. We talked about their vocational plans and their educational choices. They had visited me to express concerns about the "liberal drift" of our religion department and that of the university. They were polite and sincere in their convictions. I was grateful for the politeness that was not always common among those with strong compassions, either liberal or conservative.

Apprehensively, I listened.

"Yes. I always remember what you said one day in class, and it revolutionized my concept of ministry," Joel said. "I just want to call and say thank you."

"Perhaps we can get together for lunch someday soon," I said. I knew Joel lived not too far from his alma mater and my place of employment.

"Let's do that," he said, friendly in his tone.

We never did get together for lunch. I have often wondered what I said that revolutionized his concept of ministry. What could I have said that would make an impression on one whom I never imagined I had much impact? I have a reasonable guess, but I may never know. Perhaps I don't want to know. Not knowing keeps me wondering what I have taught and will teach that might be caught by some fellow traveler.

## Questions to Ponder

1. Have you ever had a positive impact on someone only to learn about it years later? Explain.

2. What would you imagine Joel took away from his classroom experience with the author?

3. Can individuals with differing theological orientations communicate with each other? Explain.

# God of All Who Would Learn

God of all who would learn and all who would teach, show us how to honor those who teach and to encourage those who would learn. For their time invested in study and preparation, we give thanks; for their time spent in willingness to learn and to take chances, we give thanks. Growing in learning means growing in applying that learning. Scripture teaches that genuine biblical learning and subsequent doing are intertwined. May these demands of discipleship not be foreign to us in everyday life.

We claim you as the designer of all knowledge and wisdom. Wisdom and knowledge belong to you. You have created us with human minds capable of inquiry into our world. We want to know. We can explain much, but there remains much that we cannot explain. Lead us in the wisdom of knowing the difference. Remove any fear we may have of learning. All genuine learning should lead us to you.

We honor our past and present teachers by committing ourselves to the best of their teaching and recommitting to opportunities to learn and grow in our discipleship. Guide us in a deeper understanding of you. Let our learning unite us with one another. Help us in the coming days to honor the teaching of the one called Rabbi Jesus of Nazareth, Jesus the Christ. Let us walk with each other in the knowledge and fellowship of the one true God. In the name of Jesus the Crucified, we pray. Amen.

# TIMES OF THANKSGIVING

*O give thanks unto the LORD, for he is good: for his mercy endureth for ever.
Let the redeemed of the LORD say so, whom he hath redeemed from the hand
of the enemy; And gathered them out of the lands, from the east, and from the
west, from the north, and from the south.*
—Psalm 107:1-3


*When gratitude has become a matter of reasoning there are many ways of
escaping from its bonds.*
—George Eliot


*If you see no reason for giving thanks, the fault lies in yourself.*
—Minquas saying

One of the common experiences in American churches and society is the celebration of Thanksgiving. This simple family celebration is a favorite of many. Soon after the observance of Thanksgiving comes the busy month of December with the frenzy of preparations for Christmas Day. Often consisting of a family meal or a congregational meal, Thanksgiving offers a simple and unhurried time for fellowship and renewal. Often out-of-town guests, including college students, return to their home church.

Regardless of ethnocentrism, celebrations of thanksgiving are not a uniquely American experience. Like their neighbors, the Jewish people of the Old Testament celebrated various agricultural events, associated with religious activities. Times of giving thanks, with feasts and festivities, have occurred worldwide for the bounty of harvest, for a successful hunt, or for military victory. In 1621, the Pilgrims along with friendly Native Americans celebrated a bounty harvest. In 1863, President Lincoln declared a National Day of Thanksgiving to be celebrated on the last Thursday in November. In 1939, under President Franklin D. Roosevelt's administration, the celebration was moved to the fourth Thursday in November.

Thanksgiving allows an opportunity for a congregation to remember the blessings of life and the year. Communal meals offer opportunities for members to bring their favorite cooked foods. Joint meals may be held with other local churches. Outreach may occur though the celebrating of Thanksgiving. Ideally, Thanksgiving provides a concrete way to celebrate individual attitudes of gratitude within community.

The following pages provide supplemental resources that might enhance the preparation for the celebration of Thanksgiving. You will find several hymns, readings, theological reflections, and a seasonal prayer. May these resources become a seasoning to add new flavor to this important celebration. May you experience new imaginations, insights, and actions.

## The Lord We Love

**Claude Douglas Bryan**

**Suggested Tunes: DIX
RATISBON
READHED No. 76
Meter: 7.7.7.7.7.7.**

For the passing of this day, for the challenge faced this year,
Nature's fire and fury rage, rumblings circling earth's frail sphere,
Thankful for the Lord we love, Love comforts from above.

For the problems of today, for the struggles we must face,
Calling forth our deepest faith, knowing it's through God's grace,
Thankful for the Lord we love, Love comforts from above.

Hearing news beyond belief, lives will never be the same;
For the grave and worst displayed, we are filled with human shame;
Thankful for the Lord we love, Love comforts from above.

Struggles show our hidden self, selfish battles we must fight;
Now transformed by God's power, we will find God's true delight;
Thankful for the Lord we love, Love comforts from above.

# Hear Our Words of Praise and Glory

**Claude Douglas Bryan**

**Suggested Tune: HOLY MANNA**
**Meter: 8.7.8.7. with Refrain**

Hear our words of praise and glory,
Lord of Heaven, Lord of Earth,
Call to join their pilgrim story—
Matriarch and Patriarch.
God extends a life of calling,
Fellowship with God to dwell;
Walking upright keeps from falling;
Old life bid our last farewell.

Loving God is first in labor,
First in time and first in life;
Second, love for self and neighbor,
First and second yields no strife.
God extends a life of calling,
Fellowship with God to dwell;
Walking upright keeps from falling;
Old life bid our last farewell.

Joy and thanks we sing for faith's
  call
Prophets told the Savior's birth
Keep us close and true, lest we fall
Spread this message through the
  earth
God extends a life of calling,
Fellowship with God to dwell;
Walking upright keeps from falling;
Old life bid our last farewell.

Gratitude for life eternal;
Living daily through the Son;
Love makes life and work supernal;
Living life the Savior won.
God extends a life of calling,
Fellowship with God to dwell;
Walking upright keeps from falling;
Old life bid our last farewell.

# Thanksgiving (Responsive Reading)

LEADER: Our Father, forgive us for not being thankful. We should not need a specific day to remind us to give thanks for our blessings and most of all for your Son.

**PEOPLE:** Our Father, on this day of Thanksgiving, may we truly give thanks for the simple gifts of life which we often take for granted and for the most precious gift, your Son.

LEADER: Our Father, not only do we thank you for the roast turkey, the cranberry sauce, and pumpkin pies, but we thank and praise you for eternal life in your Son.

**PEOPLE:** Our Father, grant us the spirit not only to celebrate your goodness on this Thanksgiving Day, but also each day may we sing and shout of your eternal grace. May each day be a day of thanks for your giving.

LEADER: Our Father, may we not be misers of your love and mere keepers of your faith, but may we give our love as we receive it from you and share our faith with those around us. May we share the bounty of our spiritual and physical blessings with those in need.

**PEOPLE:** Our Father, as we turn to those around us and give thanks for their presence with us, may this be a time of praising and sharing your love with our brothers and sisters.

LEADER: So many times, we give monetary offerings during worship services. In the next few moments let us give the greatest offering of all— our love. As we feel led, let us go to those around us, those in the center of the group and those in the lonely corners of the room, and express to each how much they mean to us.

 

# Thanksgiving (Poem)

Thanksgiving, a human response to acts of grace,
Seeing, recognizing, and appreciating,
Not by human work and pursuit alone,
Found through God's grace and mercy.

Thanksgiving greater than the Pilgrim's Story,
Though all pilgrims viewed from celestial heights;
Everywhere working, waiting, watching, and wanting,
Celebrating gains they cannot accomplish alone.

Thanksgiving begins in knowing we are not a god,
Beloved creature subject to the Creator's design;
Within this sphere, given what we cannot create,
Though alone, we know God's kindness and care

Thanksgiving held with bounds of fellowship,
Directed to God the Creator and the Sustainer;
Heads bowed, eyes closed and hands holding hands,
Silence and voice leading hearts and minds as one.

True Thanksgiving comes after the meals have ceased,
When we return to who we daily are,
Showing compassion, sharing, accepting, and listening;
True Thanksgiving lives beyond the gathered meal.

## Questions to Ponder

1. Is thanksgiving a response to grace? Explain.
2. Is thanksgiving a worldwide phenomenon? If so, why?
3. What does the author mean when he says "true thanksgiving lives beyond the gathered meal"?
4. What are the takeaways from the poem?

# Noreen's Words

Graduation Day had been wonderful for Jessica, having graduated college with honors. Last farewells to graduating friends and to friends who had not yet graduated had created emotional upheavals. They recalled memories and exchanged best wishes. Jessica's parents helped in relocating her belongings to her home for a temporary stay. In several months, she would be leaving for graduate school. This summer would be the last one home before leaving for the other side of the country.

Now her summer spent working with the church youth was concluding. The last evening worship service was held. She had received praises and accolades from the pastor, the youth, and the youth's parents and grandparents. As she prepared to go to the fellowship hall where a special farewell party was being held in her honor, Jessica stopped by the organ where the eighty-plus-year-old organist played.

The organist, known as Miss Noreen to the congregation, stood up. Noreen had been the organist for sixty years and had played for three generations of church members. Noreen turned to Jessica and said in her deep and sweet Southern accent, "Darling, you've received lots of praise and compliments throughout your summer here, helping with the youth activities. I've witnessed this happen for sixty-plus years in this church. I want to tell you something that I hope you will remember. As you go on in life, you're going to receive lots of praises and congratulations on your accomplishments. All of that is good. Be grateful for what you have and what you can do. But, when you are praised, patted on the back, or hugged for how good you did, let it go to your heart and not to your head. Let the praise settle and enlarge your heart and not your head. God knows we got plenty of big-headed people. I see them from where I sit every Sunday and Wednesday night. We need more folks with big hearts." Both smiled at each other.

"Now for the peach ice cream. Let's go," Miss Noreen said.

## Questions to Ponder

1. What was Noreen's fear for Jessica?
2. What impact should praise have on our lives?
3. Can you both give praise and receive praise?

 

# Mighty Mite

I suspect that members of my small church would have regarded eighteen-year-old me as spiritually mature for my age. It was not that they had watched me through the years. I came to them late as a seventeen-year-old, only weeks after my high school graduation. I came to the church for baptism and membership. I was consistent in my attendance each Sunday, even when coming home every weekend from a state university. They loved, accepted, and supported me. I could not imagine being without them, especially for my first year of college. I enjoyed being around the adults, especially the older adults, who became like aunts and uncles and grandmas and grandpas to me.

One of my church aunts approached me after the worship service and said, "I brought you something back from my trip to Israel."

Immediately, I thought of what the gift might be. An olive wood statue, a nativity scene, or a Jewish religious article? What would it be?

She pulled from her coat pocket her treasure and placed it in my open palm. I looked at it and remember her words: "It's a widow's mite, like the one mentioned in the Bible. Of course, it is a replica."

I examined the coin, smiled, and responded, "Thank you. I'll remember you and the gift." While I said the right words, a completely different dramatic monologue played in my head. *You traveled thousands of miles to Israel, and this is what you brought me back? Couldn't you have brought me something bigger and better? Maybe you should just keep it.*

Thanks be to God that I did not declare my inner monologue.

Within a few days after reflecting on my unspoken thoughts and continuing for years later, I was and have been ashamed of my superficial "inner monologue." Outwardly I might have appeared mature, but inwardly I was immature, pure and simple. My thoughts had violated the very spirit sought to be conveyed by the biblical widow who gave what she had. I was like the other biblical onlookers who witnessed her act and responded negatively.

This woman's gift has long been lost in my own travels and relocations. The memory remains, as the coin was not the real gift, but the real gift was in my reflections on my immaturity. While not always practiced consistently, I try to look upon gifts for what they are and not for what I want to them to be. More importantly, I ask myself, have I given my best in service, in compassion, and in understanding to others? When I do, I experience moments of genuine thanksgiving.

## Questions to Ponder

1. Have inner, unspoken thoughts conflicted with your spoken words? Explain.
2. What role do our inner monologues or dialogues play in our growth and development?
3. What contributes to the way we think and act?
4. How can we develop genuine thanksgiving?

# God of the Sowing

God of the sowing, the nurturing, and the harvesting, we thank you for the bounty of food we experience, for the housing we have, for the neighborhoods we live in, for the friendship and families we enjoy, and for the beauty of our place of worship. Help us to share this bounty with others who might appear less affluent and advantaged. May any privilege of affluence we possess cause us to assume responsibility for the less fortunate, those whose birth provided limited accessibility for growth, opportunity, and comfort. Remove any ill will or condescension we might have as we give to others. Help us to remember that because of you we are blessed so that we might bless others.

We thank you for many gifts but especially for expressions of your love. We cannot escape your love. May this love received challenge us to become Jesus' love incarnate for our world. Show us the roles we should play in your heavenly harvest. Whether we sow, water, wait, or harvest, may we walk our path with the joy of new beginnings for all of creation. Your mercy we praise. In the name of Jesus the Crucified, we pray. Amen.

# TIMES OF WEDDINGS AND MARRIAGES

*What therefore God hath joined together, let not man put asunder.*
—Mark 10:9

*Love doesn't make the world go round;*
*love is what makes the ride worthwhile.*
—Elizabeth Barrett Browning

*There is no more lovely, friendly and charming relationship,*
*communion or company than a good marriage.*
—Martin Luther

*The ornament of a house is the friends who frequent it.*
—Ralph Waldo Emerson

Nationally, weddings are a big business, with some individuals investing tens of thousands of dollars or more into elaborate church weddings and destination weddings. One of the celebratory moments in congregational life is a wedding. Weddings have become more complicated as views on who can marry have undergone debate and polarization. Pastors, other ordained ministers, families, friends, and congregants are caught up in the chaos. It is beyond the scope of this work to address these moral or ethical questions.

When the decision to hold a wedding ceremony occurs, thought and planning go into the event. Circumstances may indicate adaptations. Weddings can be a mixture of eclectic practices observed at other weddings, depicted in magazines, or shown in films.

Before the wedding occurs, pastoral care and counseling should be extended to the couple. Helping them to discuss what Christian marriage involves, the challenges they may face, and the future relationships with in-laws is critical.

The following pages provide supplemental resources that might enhance the preparation for the celebration of weddings. You will find several hymns, readings, stories and theological reflections, and a seasonal prayer. May these resources become a seasoning to add new flavor to this important celebration. May you experience new imaginations, insights, and actions.

# A Wedding Vow, A Sacred One

**Claude Douglas Bryan**　　　　　　**Suggested Tunes: CANONBURY**
　　　　　　　　　　　　　　　　　　　　　　　　**WALTHAM**
　　　　　　　　　　　　　　　　　　**Meter: 8.8.8.8.**

A wedding vow, a sacred one,
These holy pledges shall be kept,
Through good and bad, till life is done
What they have vowed, we each accept.

God bless the ones who join this day,
In love and faith they pledge these two—
To seek thy will and to obey;
Grant grace and strength to follow through.

Transform these families as one;
Respect the past, yet move ahead;
Renew, remind each, of the Son,
Who offers each the Living Bread.

We witness vows they make today,
Support and love we give to guide
Along this family's new way,
May love and peace grow ever wide.

# Lighting the Candles

**Claude Douglas Bryan**

**Suggested Tunes: BEECHER
CASSELL
Meter: 8.7.8.7.D.**

Loving Father, bless our gath'ring,
Welcoming each one today;
Friend and family bring their
  greeting;
Love and union call this way.
May we put away distractions
That divert and change our
  thoughts.
Minds and hearts on loving actions
Following what God has taught.

Moments sacred call for praising;
Gracious Lord we claim thy name;
Songs of heaven joyful raising,
Lasting love, abiding claim.
Once more, fill us, Holy Spirit,
Transform ev'ryone today;
Growing power of thy Spirit
Leads us all each day to pray.

Parents come to light the candles,
Showing each the child they bring;
Memories engulf these candles,
Lullabies that they would sing.
Tears and laughter, joys of parents,
Precious childhood they recall;
Letting go, the call of parents,
Blessings give support to all.

Children come, no longer children,
Lighting candles, flames of life;
Young and fearless, still our
  children,
Hopeful futures without strife.
Bless and guard them to each other,
Building lives, becoming one;
Keep them faithful to one another,
Till their life and love are done.

## A Wedding Welcome and Hope (Greeting)

Our Creator, we praise your name as the Great I Am. We gather on this occasion to celebrate the marriage of ____________ and ____________ and their respective families who will be part of this new union. As Jesus celebrated at the wedding at Cana, we celebrate as well.

Bless these individuals in this new journey of faith. Give them love and patience with one another. Help them to nurture their love and commitment to one another in the coming years. Help them to learn and to change from any mistakes they may make both intentionally and unintentionally. Let this marriage commitment be an exciting challenge and venture for them. May they grow as individuals and grow as a couple in similar directions. May we provide them with the friendship of family to assist them and to support them in their public commitment to one another.

May other marriage vows be renewed quietly, as we are privileged to witness this new commitment. Fill us each with the grace necessary for living responsibly in your Kingdom. Let us welcome each other to this commitment of love and devotion. Amen.

 

# Marriage (Benediction)

God, we thank you for these two individuals. May we have listened to your Spirit. May we be challenged, by their commitment, to lead better lives. Lead us to live lives of integrity, of virtue, of patience, and of compassion. Thank you for this couple and their public declaration of love and commitment to one another. In the coming days strengthen their bond with one another. Out of that love may their witness be clear.

Guide us as we leave both in joy and in reflection, identifying our commitment, our loyalty, and our compassion for one another. In the days ahead, sometimes bright and sometimes dark, sometimes in prosperity and sometimes in poverty, in their travel, and in their return, may they receive God's presence and protection. Just as the Lord celebrated the wedding at Cana, we celebrate today this union. May they and their respective families grow in harmony and in the name of Jesus the Christ. Amen.

# Cuddling Porcupines

In college, I became acquainted with a metaphor with wonderful sustaining power. I associate the metaphor with L. D. Johnson, professor and chaplain at Furman University. Johnson described two porcupines cuddling for warmth. It was a metaphor for two people in love and in marriage. Let me extend and reflect on this metaphor. A good marriage is like two porcupines. It's a cold day. The only way they can sustain warmth is to huddle together. It takes two porcupines a long time to learn how to stay warm. If they get too close to one another, they can prick one another and cause great pain. If they are not close enough, never touching each other, they cannot enjoy the warmth of one another. Yes, like a good marriage, the two porcupines must learn to live together.

Should a new porcupine join the two porcupines, unfamiliar problems arise. Some porcupines don't serve the third intrusion, whether it be another porcupine or another loyalty. Porcupines have a lifelong battle learning how to be close enough for warmth, for protection, and for guidance. As porcupines grow, the distance and configurations must be renegotiated. When little porcupines join the mix, relationships must be renegotiated. When the offspring porcupine becomes an adult seeking another porcupine, the original two porcupines must renegotiate their boundaries once more.

## Questions to Ponder

1. Can two people be too close? Explain.
2. What happens if they are not close at all?
3. Does marriage involve pain? Explain.

 

# Pursuing Character

Young adults, and sometimes would-be young adults, often find themselves preoccupied with issues of "finding the right person." Historically, marriage choices were made by parents and marriage brokers for the best interests of son, daughter, family alliances, land and business alliances, and political alliances. Individualistic societal orientations often reject this collective approach in marriage decision-making. However, in fairness, who should know the individual better, and know who might have the best potential for his or her happiness, than his or her families? Families had a high stake in the marriage engagement.

Individualistic societies emphasize the primacy of the individual choice. Beginning in the twentieth century, this individualistic orientation has focused on finding the elusive right person who typically meets romantic aspects of physical attraction. Prior marriageability criteria often involved finding the "right match," which might include being a good provider, offering stability, having similarity of faith orientations, having the ability to produce children, having good financial prospects and good social standing. While these criteria remain important to many, often the main criteria involve the high priority of physical and emotional attraction.

As a teacher who perpetually referenced Erik Erickson's Eight Stages of Man, I led class discussion on the "Identity Versus Role Confusion" and "Intimacy Versus Isolation" tasks. Identity should precede intimacy, I stressed. How can you know someone else if you do not know yourself?

Admittedly, I often struggled with the popular concept of knowing the "Mind of Christ" without knowing your own mind. As I repeatedly told my students, don't focus exclusive energies on finding the right person. Instead, focus energy on becoming and being the right person. If we can find integrity with who we are, we then have the potential for finding the right person. Focus on your identity, including important aspects of social and faith identity. Ask and find answers about yourself prior to asking for or agreeing to marriage. Put yourself in places suitable for expressing and discovering your identity. Let us seek to be and to look for people of character, not just look for a character.

## Questions to Ponder

1. Should identity precede intimacy? Explain.
2. Does identity formation stop with marriage? Explain.
3. What makes for success in marriage? Explain.
4. How important is character in relationships? Explain.

# God of Love and Commitment

God of love and commitment shown in the birth, life, death, and resurrection of Jesus the Christ, bless those who have already committed themselves in marriage and those who come today to join in marriage supported by community. Jesus was a guest at the wedding at Cana. Jesus, be our guest today. We invite you into these celebrations.

Join these two [insert names] before us today in the presence of family and friends as they make public vows of commitment in your presence and witness. Each of the two bring various experiences and commitments in their willingness to love, support, protect, and encourage each other. Bless their commitment to one of the most powerful human relationships. Within this circle of commitment, each one possesses the ability to bring out the best or the worst in each other. We pray that their desire by their words and behaviors would be to bring out the best in one another.

May all our human relationships be strengthened by their witness today. Help us to provide a community of support in which their lives will be encouraged through the easy and the difficult changes that we all face. Help them to flourish and to give encouragement to others through their mutual commitment. Let each one present honor God first. Help this couple to give primary focus to their relationship with one another. If they can love one another, this love will be translated into other relationships, including love for you and others. Bless this sacred time of commitment. In the name of Jesus the Crucified, we pray. Amen.

# EPILOGUE

As you read these words, hopefully you have found the foregoing resources to be helpful, not only in your personal life but also in community worship. While the book's title identifies the theme of exile, we are always in exile from our ultimate destiny. We are on a journey that has its own time, place, and sacredness. God is the God of the Exile but also the God of the Pre-Exile and the After-Exile life. Exile may be a physical place, or it may be the trauma of being out of place in one's community of faith or in one's society. Exile impacts who we are and who we become. We cannot help but be impacted in some way. Old ideas may be reinforced or new ideas may be found. Exile changes us. We find new signs of both exits and entrances.

We are called to be creative and dynamic, to grow in all our relationships, regardless of where we are. Limitations can be opportunities for new discoveries. Whether you are in your own uncomfortable Babylon or in your own comfortable hometown, may you find God in both the journey and the destination.